"I've known Todd for many years and have been so encouraged by his deep love for the Lord and for his family. In his new book, *Weak Is the New Strong*, Todd shows us how, through Christ, *anything* is possible. Our weaknesses are not useless to God; they are where his power can work the most!"

> —**Robert Morris,** Founding Lead Senior Pastor of Gateway Church, and best-selling author of *The Blessed Life, Beyond Blessed,* and *Take the Day Off*

"My friend Todd Lollar knows that God's power is revealed in the most peculiar ways. The things we tend to be ashamed of often become the very things God uses to redeem the world, and the scars that show what we have survived can become our credentials. You are going to love this book. Todd is one of the bright lights in this world."

> —**Shane Claiborne,** author, activist, and Cofounder of Red Letter Christians

"In a book full of fire, gentleness, and generosity, Todd Lollar showcases how weakness is a strength and how woundedness makes us whole. In the same way adding impurities to a material like aluminum strengthens and stiffens it, since pure aluminum is too soft to be of any use on its own, so weakness is the secret sauce of greatness and power. Maybe it's time for a weakness—not just strengths—inventory."

> —**Leonard Sweet,** best-selling author of *Rings of Fire,* and Founder and president of SpiritVenture Ministries

"*Weak Is the New Strong* is a timely message for a world distracted from the things that really matter. Todd Lollar uses lessons from his life filled with challenge, disappointment, and heartbreak to show us all that there is strength in our weakness, joy in our pain, and beauty in our brokenness."

> —**Patrick Gray and Justin Skeesuck,** authors of *I'll Push You* and *Imprints: The Evidence Our Lives Leave Behind*

"I have known Todd for over twenty years. He was the first person to disciple me as a new believer in college, and he eventually became my roommate, ministry associate, and dear friend. Todd lives his faith like few I know. His physical weakness has formed a strength and resolve that transforms anyone who meets him. Todd's life is a profound message that Jesus is alive and ready to love us, change us, and empower us, no matter what confronts us in this life. This book will give you insight into the power of the gospel and how the power of Christ is made for our weakness."

—**Michael Miller,** Founder and Senior Pastor of UPPERROOM

"My friend Todd Lollar's constant kindness towards others is a shining example of the love Jesus has for us all. Todd's weaknesses have not kept him from working hard and chasing his dreams. Todd is a rock star—bold and brave, he shows through his life that God's power is made perfect in weakness. The truth is we are all weak. *Weak Is the New Strong* is such an inspiration, and it has encouraged me to no longer hide my weaknesses, but to see them as a lampstand for displaying God's power. Like your favorite song, you'll want to put this book's message on repeat in your daily life."

—**Aaron Watson,** singer and songwriter

"I've been fortunate to know Todd for many years. His love and passion for the Lord is clear, as evidenced in the words written on these pages. Todd's book gave me pause. It brought tears to my eyes, a smile to my face—it helped soften the parts of me that I've worked hard to armor up. I'm honored to be his friend and to share this book with my friends!"

—**Alecia Davis,** TV personality and host, *Extra* and CMT

"We all have weaknesses, though some of us have the ability to hide them better than others. In *Weak Is the New Strong*, Todd Lollar shows us not only how to not feel compelled to hide those weaknesses, but also how God can use our weaknesses to perfect us. There's strength in weakness, and Todd helps us see that good news."

—**Luke Norsworthy,** author of *Befriending Your Monsters* and host of the *Newsworthy with Norsworthy* podcast

"While reading this poignant, convicting book, I was reminded of a weekly scene at our church while Todd was in seminary: he was always surrounded by people. Both young and old were drawn to his radical kindness, his wisdom, and his pace. Todd's words invite us into a world where our identity is anchored in God's assurance that his grace is sufficient for us."

—**Mike Cope,** Director of Ministry Outreach, Pepperdine University

FOREWORD BY
JASE ROBERTSON

Weak
Is the
New
Str ng

God's Perfect   Power in You

TODD LOLLAR

LEAFWOOD
PUBLISHERS
an imprint of Abilene Christian University Press

To my wife, Marissa,
who makes unmerited favor realized

WEAK IS THE NEW STRONG

God's Perfect Power in You

L E A F W O O D
P U B L I S H E R S

an imprint of Abilene Christian University Press

Copyright © 2020 by Todd Lollar

ISBN: 987-1-68426-051-5 | LCCN 2020004985

Printed in the United States of America

LIBRARY OF CONGRESS CATALOGING-IN-PUBLICATION DATA
Names: Lollar, Todd, author.
Title: Weak is the new strong : God's perfect power in you / Todd Lollar.
Description: Abilene : Leafwood Publishers, 2020. | Includes
    bibliographical references.
Identifiers: LCCN 2020004985 | ISBN 9781684260515 (paperback)
Subjects: LCSH: Cerebral palsy—Patients—Religious life. |
    Self-acceptance—Religious aspects—Christianity.
Classification: LCC BV4910.333 L65 2020 | DDC 248.8/61968360092—dc23
LC record available at https://lccn.loc.gov/2020004985

Cover design by ThinkPen Design | Interior text design by Sandy Armstrong, Strong Design

Leafwood Publishers is an imprint of Abilene Christian University Press
ACU Box 29138, Abilene, Texas 79699

1-877-816-4455 | www.leafwoodpublishers.com

20 21 22 23 24 25 / 7 6 5 4 3 2

CONTENTS

Foreword by Jase Robertson.. 9

Chapter 1: Child of Weakness 13

Chapter 2: Imprisoned by Weakness.................................. 29

Chapter 3: Weakness Redefined.. 45

Chapter 4: Transparent Weakness Opens Doors 61

Chapter 5: A Weak Prayer to Meet Bono........................... 81

Chapter 6: Weakness Destroys Barriers............................. 99

Chapter 7: Today's Weakness Is Tomorrow's Encouragement.. 117

Chapter 8: Lack Is the New More...................................... 135

Chapter 9: Weakness in Community 155

Chapter 10: Pass On the Power 173

Acknowledgments... 191

FOREWORD

I met Todd in Southlake, Texas, at Gateway Church a few years ago. Pastor Robert Morris had asked me to speak at a men's event for the church, and the experience there brought many to Jesus and created eternal friendships. There would be other events at Gateway for me and members of my family, but this event was special because it was the first and it was where I met Todd and his family. As we got to know each other, it became clear that God had orchestrated our meeting. Among God's many talents, he is really good at bringing people together.

The "chance" meeting happened as a result of Todd's reputation. The day before I left for Gateway, a buddy of mine called me and said "I heard you are going to Southlake, Texas, and you *must* meet Todd Lollar. He shares Jesus as much as, or even more than, you and your dad." That got my attention because my dad is Phil Robertson. My dad has been sharing Jesus to everyone within earshot since I was a teenager. The only other thing my friend told me about Todd was that they met at Louisiana State University and Todd had shared Jesus with him even though he was already a believer. I am a huge LSU fan, and I've been to enough football games to know that college campuses really need Jesus. Geaux Tigers! I asked my assistant to coordinate letting Todd and his family into the green room before I was to speak. When Todd rolled in (literally) with his family, my first thought was: the Lord uses those we least suspect. I was also reminded of 1 Samuel 16:7: "The Lord does not look at the things people look at. People look at the outward appearance, but the Lord looks at the heart."

Todd and I have stayed in touch over the years, and I am excited you are reading this book. Todd reminds me so much of the blind man in John 9 who met Jesus and had his life transformed. In the story, the religious onlookers were bombarding Jesus with questions of "why this happened" and who was "to blame for this." Jesus ignored their questions and focused everyone's attention on what *he* was going to do about it! John 9:3 says, "this happened so that the work of God will be displayed in his life."

This book is about God using our weakness as his strength. When Todd sent me this book, I read it from start to finish in one sitting. I could not put it down. It is real, useful, and inspirational, with a touch of humor. It is motivational to see a man who has endured so much pain, frustration, and challenge in his life have such a sense of humor woven through his God-transformed character. The irony of meeting Todd at a speaking event is that my biggest weakness has always been shyness and public speaking. God changed that into a strength! It is what God does.

I am honored to know Todd and his beautiful family, and I wholeheartedly support what he has written in this book. He is a friend, brother, and partner in Jesus. Todd has had more than enough reasons to complain or give up in life, but God transformed him. Todd is a son of God, a disciple of Jesus, and a Spirit-filled warrior. God can transform you too—and Jesus endured a cross to prove it. Jesus rose from the grave so that we can rise every day in confidence despite our struggles, which God will continue to turn into strengths. Enjoy this book and the transformation God brings with it.

Your partner in Jesus,
Jase Robertson
Author and speaker from A&E's *Duck Dynasty*

CHAPTER 1

CHILD OF WEAKNESS

"I hear the Savior say
Thy strength indeed is small
Child of weakness, watch and pray
Find in Me thine all in all."
—Elvina M. Hall, "Jesus Paid It All"

My life nearly ended just as it began.

Seconds after I was born, blue-faced and barely breathing, the doctors rushed me out of the delivery room and put me on oxygen.

While I was struggling to live, my mother pleaded with God for my life. She shed no tears of fear or hopelessness. Rather, she trusted her creator. God calmed her soul and reassured her I would live. (Years later, he would fully answer her two-part prayer on my behalf.)

Sometime that same night, they took me off oxygen. I was allowed to go home just like any other normal baby.

Except, I was anything but normal.

When I was a few months old, my mother realized something was different about my physical development. She took me to a doctor who said, "He's fine. He's just a fat, lazy baby."

But at nine months, I couldn't hold my head up by myself. I couldn't sit alone. My mother took me to another doctor whose best guess at diagnosing me was "developmental retardation." He warned my mom of the possibility that I would never walk, talk, or learn.

But I still had undiagnosed developmental issues. At eighteen months, I saw a specialist at the JD McCarty Center for Children with Developmental Disabilities in Norman, Oklahoma. Just when other almost–two-year-olds were growing stronger and learning to walk so they could run, I was diagnosed with cerebral palsy.

My Weakness

Without knowing it, you may have met someone with cerebral palsy (CP) before. You may have met someone who seemed different, but you didn't know why and you were afraid to ask. If you don't know someone with CP, it's hard to know what to say, and it's twice as hard to know what their daily life is like.

Cerebral palsy is most often caused by a brain injury before, during, or right after birth. It affects a person's ability to control their muscles, but it affects each person differently and to different degrees. Some people with CP may not be able to control their left arm movements. Others may struggle to control multiple muscles, including those used for speech. Some suffer from partial to total paralysis.

The best way I can describe having CP is to imagine that each affected muscle has a mind of its own and seldom, if ever, listens to the mind in your head.

CP is non-life-threatening, but it is a life sentence. There is no earthly cure—only different therapies for physical, speech, and occupational help. CP is not a disease, but it affects everyday life. This is even more apparent in the face of obstacles such as no ramp access for a person with CP who must use a wheelchair—like me.

Cerebral palsy does not worsen with time like some neurological conditions, but it could if I chose to give up. I will always have as "much" CP as I do now; but through various kinds of therapy, I can lessen its effects on my daily life. In fact, I can even get better if I stay active. For instance, even though I have a speech disfluency that causes me to speak slowly and with a stutter, it was much worse when I was a child through my collegiate days.

I don't define myself through CP; but because its effects are so evident in my life, that's how most people define me: by my greatest weakness. And I've had to live with this perception for my entire life.

Imagine being publicly defined by *your* greatest weakness.

That's not such a thrilling prospect, is it?

Fighting the Misperception of Struggling with CP

Unless you know someone with cerebral palsy, daily life with CP is different than what you may think. When living with CP, these misperceptions are more detrimental than the realities.

For instance, some people believe I don't do much because I have to use a wheelchair. I chuckle when I hear this—especially when it's uttered by someone who's seen or experienced the results of my work but didn't see me actually doing the work. This misperception generally comes from older generations, whose limited notions of the potential of wheelchair-bound people are based on decades long past when people like me weren't given opportunities to accomplish, achieve, and live out their calling. They seem to believe that people in wheelchairs have only two options: stay at home with Mom and Dad or live in a group home of other wheelchair-bound people. So, when they see me active and independent, it's surprising.

Older generations think I'm an adult who's still dependent on his parents or some caretaker. They're surprised when they learn

I moved out of my parents' house at nineteen to attend college at the University of Oklahoma. They're even more surprised when they hear I later earned a master's in biblical and related studies.

Following my graduate work, I moved to the Dallas-Fort Worth Metroplex, while all of my family still lived in Oklahoma. Yet because of my perceived weaknesses, people seem to believe that my family must have a major supportive role in my life. They do support me, but in the same ways that all good family members support each other: with love and help—when needed.

Lastly, some people believe I have low aspirations. This is frustrating for a leader who likes to think he has a great, God-given vision for seeing God transform lives throughout cities, who also pioneered and leads an expanding nonprofit organization, and who's a certified life coach.

When I'm unloading my wheelchair out of my Jeep, I've heard people exclaim, "Wow! You're out and about!" or, "You do well for yourself, don't you?" Their eyes seem to bulge in a mixture of shock, disbelief, and pity, as if my goal for the day was just to get my wheelchair out of my Jeep! Consequently, I feel like I'm sometimes not taken seriously when I talk about vision. I fear that others see my disability and automatically set the bar low on my behalf, as if I don't have lofty goals for my career, my family, and my life.

Those are my main frustrations in living with CP, and I don't begrudge people who hold misperceptions about my life. They just don't know what it's like inside my mind, either because they've never known someone like me or because they just don't have the time to talk—which leads me to the realities of my day-to-day life.

Living with CP

I am mobilized in a wheelchair. I specifically use that phrase because I am not totally or partially paralyzed. I could walk with a cane or walker if I chose to, but I choose not to. Why? Because my calling in life is to make a difference in other people's lives, and I've discovered that society seems to be more accepting of someone approaching them in a wheelchair than someone who's struggling to approach them. That's the practical reason. More personally, my desire to help others far exceeds my desire to walk. Far from being a two-wheeled straitjacket for my legs, my wheelchair frees me to do life.

Another issue I must daily deal with is my speed. Even though my physical challenges have drastically improved as I've aged, one reality remains: I'm slow. I talk slowly. I move slowly. I do not get things done even close to as fast as you do. I've adapted, but my all-around slowness is still apparent, especially when I roll next to a friend on a walk. My gifts are much more relational—and slow. This slowness is an asset. Effective leadership isn't about how much you can get done; it's about how much of an impact you make. That doesn't require speed.

It's also amazing to see how God works when we just . . . slow . . . down. I've often noticed that people who claim to be too busy may be purposefully busy because they're running away from deeper pain. They fill their time with things to do and places to be, and so God can't speak into the empty silence of their hidden hurt. I've seen the roots of such pain come into the light of Christ's healing simply because someone was forced to slow down when they spoke with me.

Culture says, "Don't just sit there. Do something."

My life teaches, "Don't just do something. Sit there."

The most fulfilling vision I've gained in leadership and life has come from slowing down my mind. In this case, the speed of my body is often a good goal to which to slow my mind.

There's only one part of me that isn't slow: my mind. I think like The Flash compared to how slowly I speak. This impacts me in different ways. For instance, people must slow down to hear me out. The ones who do, seem to think it's more than worth the extra time. They'll even say something about how nice it was to "stop and smell the roses" when talking with me, because they're so used to our fast-paced culture. Really, what they're saying is that it's life-changing in the moment to stop and realize what life is about.

> The most fulfilling vision I've gained in leadership and life has come from slowing down my mind.

Problems arise when a person begins talking to me, and, in less than five seconds, assumes I have a mental disorder and makes no attempt to hear me out. I just keep talking until I press through their misconceptions of my mind. I keep talking to help them understand what I'm trying to convey. I have patience for them, because I know it requires patience to hear me out. Often, thankfully, this initial, close-minded reaction disappears once they understand my words and my heart.

Still . . . our microwave culture . . . of instant everything . . . doesn't tolerate . . . slowness of speech . . . very well . . . just like you . . . might be getting tired . . . of how this sentence . . . is written. Can you imagine . . . if I'd written . . . this whole book . . . thiiiiiiis way?

You may not have kept reading.

My greatest struggle in living with CP is the belief that I have to prove myself to everyone. (Isn't this a struggle for us all?) Because I'm so aware of my limitations, particularly with my lack of speed in movement and speech, I default to thinking that I have to prove myself in *every* area of my life. This isn't conducive to a peaceful, worry-free life. And it's certainly exhausting: for me, for those closest to me, and for those to whom I think I need to prove myself. Through much trial and error, I've learned that people want the real you and not the person you try so hard to be in order to meet their perception of you.

To that end, my name is Todd Lollar.

I love Jesus and my family.

I can't believe my career is ministering to others, serving others, leading others, and encouraging them in their God-given purposes for their lives!

I have cerebral palsy, and I'm a picture of God's strength being made perfect in weakness.

> People want the real you and not the person you try so hard to be in order to meet their perception of you.

My day-to-day life with CP isn't easy, but it's better than it's ever been. While I'm grateful for speech therapy and physical therapy—which I haven't had to use since my college days—I truly believe that my mobility and speech have drastically improved because of believing the message of this book: God's power is made perfect in weakness!

Helpless like Me—like Us

Elvis is crooning a Christmas song from a vinyl record on my grandparents' immense console stereo. Grandma runs into the room. Just loud enough so we'd all surely hear her, she says, "Seems Grandpa forgot to pick up film today."

Dutifully, and with a not-so-hidden smile, Grandpa heads to the store.

This is the most nostalgic memory of my childhood. My grandparents seemed to run out of film every year. And every year, I couldn't believe that Grandpa would always miss out when the jingle bells rang out from the front porch, we'd all run to the front door, and Santa Claus—the jolly red man himself—was right there!

He'd hug each of us (he smelled faintly familiar), call us by name, and hand each of us a gift. But even as thrilled as I was to have Santa in my home, I'd get lost looking at another Christmas scene that was never missing from their home: the manger.

I'd stare at baby Jesus in the stable and think, *He was weak and helpless then, kind of like me now.* I'd look at my heavy, metal-laden legs, where braces covered me from the waist down. I'd think about how I stuttered and slurred my every word. I'd feel trapped in a body I'd never asked for.

God in the flesh, Jesus, was just as trapped: incredible potential in a limited body.

The fact that God willingly made himself weak by taking on human flesh is evidence of God's desire to be with us *where we are.* Emmanuel, the name Jesus is given by the angel Gabriel when he speaks to Joseph, Jesus's earthly father, attests to that fact. Emmanuel means "God with us."

Have you ever considered the immense humility God expressed to become one of us?

When Jesus was born, he was totally dependent on his parents. He was completely subject to circumstances outside of his control, which is a ridiculous statement to make when we're talking about the Creator of the universe who effectively allowed himself to be subject to his creation. Jesus also experienced all the messiness of being human, from wetting himself as a baby to enduring awkward teenage years to feeling the effects of age as he grew into a man. The Bible relates that he was born just as we are, subject to the frailty of this world: "But when the fullness of the time came, God sent forth His Son, born of a woman, born under the Law" (Gal. 4:4).

If you think you face unfathomable weakness, consider God limiting himself in human skin.

Jesus also chose to become weak like us so he could stand in on our behalf before God the Father: "Therefore, He had to be made like His brethren in all things [i.e., weak], so that He might become a merciful and faithful high priest in things pertaining to God, to make propitiation for the sins of the people" (Heb. 2:17). And the strongest man who's ever lived still had compassion for our weaknesses: "For while we were still helpless, at the right time Christ died for the ungodly" (Rom. 5:6).

God-in-the-flesh dwelled among men and women in the same inherent weakness we endure every day. Yet his power constantly revealed itself through the weaknesses he encountered, from the persistently weak faith of his disciples to the hundreds of physically weak people who sought his healing touch. For those who were open to his teaching, who learned what it meant to glorify God *in* their weaknesses rather than despite them, their lives were irrevocably changed.

What we need to know today is what I've spent my life learning: weak is the new strong.

Our Weakness

You and I are more alike than you may think. Whether you have CP or not, you were likewise born into weakness. You arrived into this world as a baby—the single most helpless being on the planet.

Every person is born into weakness! Even Jesus, being all powerful, was. It's inevitable and inescapable.

Consider this: How much power did you have to control anything when you were born? Yes, you might have been able to bend your mother's will to your bidding by wailing at just the right time, but that was your only way to communicate.

But you're not weak only when you're a baby. You remain weak for your entire life.

Even if you're the model of physical fitness, a car crash can send you to the hospital in an instant. If you're a genius, a neurological disease can wipe your memory over the course of a few years. A traumatic brain injury can do that in seconds. If you're always in control of your feelings, one unexpected phone call can result in deep anguish, hatred, fear, or sadness.

I don't necessarily want to write about such situations, because none of us wants to *be* in those situations, but those situations happen all the time; yet so many of us want to believe that our human bodies aren't as frail and fleeting as they really are. The Bible tells us differently and in multiple instances:

- "You are just a vapor that appears for a little while and then vanishes away" (James 4:14b).
- "Behold, You have made my days as handbreadths, And my lifetime as nothing in Your sight; Surely every man at his best is a mere breath" (Ps. 39:5).
- "Man is like a mere breath; His days are like a passing shadow" (Ps. 144:4).

In other words, none of us is as strong as we think we are. The message of weakness as strength hits home to every human.

Hiding behind Strength

Our greatest collective weakness is mortality. No one lives without also dying. That's morbid, I know, but it's also the truth. Still, so much of our culture, especially in America, is focused on *not* focusing on dying. We want to stay forever young. We want to stay constantly amused. We want to stay alive as long as possible. In other words, we want to prove our strength against our greatest weakness.

But, at best, we've given temporary fixes to a "problem" we're never going to solve. We hide behind the apparent strength of our medical advances so we don't have to face the fact of our inherent, lifelong weakness. In a journey of striving to be strong and remain strong in every area of life, we run into the immense roadblock of weakness. It hits us like a brick. No matter how much we focus on being strong, a weakness in some area becomes all-encompassing the more it's ignored.

Our weaknesses must be redeemed. We must allow Jesus to show us how he transforms *all* of our weaknesses into strengths. This redemption of our weaknesses is so possible that you'll no longer want to escape through temporary fixes. Rather, you'll learn to regard your weaknesses as God-given and purposeful for your life and calling.

Every person wrestles with his or her own specific weaknesses. When I talk about weaknesses, don't automatically equate that with what may be the biggest problem-area in your life. That's certainly a weakness you need to be aware of, but we all suffer from milder weaknesses that have a multiplying effect on our lives. Like rust on an abandoned car, these weaknesses slowly accrue on top of each other over time until they begin eating away at the body itself. Left unchecked and untreated, your minor weaknesses can severely damage you, given enough time:

- ◆ You define yourself by your weaknesses instead of seeing yourself through God's eyes.
- ◆ You despise your weaknesses instead of rejoicing in them.
- ◆ You see so many barriers in your relationships that you can't see over them to connect with people.
- ◆ You have big faith, but you think your prayer life is weak.
- ◆ You want to succeed in your career, but you feel inept, inexperienced, or unqualified.
- ◆ Your finances seem depleted, and you see no hope for provision.

- You want to help others, but you feel spiritually, mentally, or physically incapable.
- You love the people in your life, but you don't see or know how to bless them.

Yet we're too often taught to disavow, cover up, or eradicate these issues so that we might be "strong."

However, when we compensate for our weaknesses by only using our strengths, we'll still find that something is lacking in our lives, because we're not living 100 percent into our true identities. When you only live out your strengths, at best, you may only be living within a small portion of your full identity. When you choose to hide your weaknesses from others, you'll never be fully known.

If you don't believe my hypothesis that we're conditioned to live only in our strengths, consider this: there's not a book called *WeakFinder*. Rather, *StrengthsFinder 2.0* is a perennial bestseller business book because it teaches people how to daily thrive in their gifts.

But what do we *do* with our weaknesses in life?

Our Perfect, Marvelous Weaknesses

If the Kryptonite always lives within us, how can we ever fly like Superman? If we're all born into weakness, where's the hope? Why should we try to discover and even rejoice in our weaknesses?

Because God calls us perfectly made.

When David, the king of ancient Israel, praised God, he wrote, "Thank you for making me so wonderfully complex! Your workmanship is marvelous—how well I know it" (Ps. 139:14 NLT). David wasn't looking into a mirror and admiring the view. Rather, he was worshiping God for God's intimate involvement in creating humanity. The verses that surround that psalm speak to how God was there when David was formed in his mother's womb—when David was in his weakest state.

Being wonderfully made astounds me. Like you may be, I'm well aware of my weaknesses, frailties, mess-ups, and failures. I've read my Bible enough and have talked to Jesus enough to have a pretty good picture of what my life ought to look like; but seldom do I live out that example in everything I say and do. So how can I, Todd Lollar, be wonderfully made, especially with so much of my physical weakness occurring so quickly after my birth?

And how can David, a man who ordered a soldier to be killed so he could sleep with that soldier's wife, call himself God's "marvelous workmanship"? How can such failures be deemed "marvelous"?

A blind man's encounter with Jesus answers the question.

Why We're All Born into Weakness

"As [Jesus] passed by, He saw a man blind from birth" (John 9:1). I'm awestruck by those first four words. Although Christ was on a mission to save humankind, he was still aware of those "he passed by." As the earthly incarnation of God, Jesus represents the love and intention God has for all his children. God does not overlook the weak. He sees you; and not only that, but he acts on what he sees. God's compassion is often engaged through weakness.

> God's compassion is often engaged through weakness.

Jesus's answer to his disciples' naive question ("Who sinned . . . that he would be born blind?" [v. 2]) is *our* answer as to why we're all born into weakness: "It was neither that this man sinned, nor his parents; *but it was so that the works of God might be displayed in him*" (John 9:3—emphasis mine). Jesus refocuses the disciples on God. He opens the disciples' eyes to a greater truth about weakness by bluntly stating why our frailties ought to be celebrated rather than mitigated.

One fascinating aspect of this story is that the man born blind doesn't ask Jesus to help him. Maybe the man spoke up and it just wasn't recorded. Maybe the man simply lifted his head when he heard Jesus and the disciples approaching and stretched out a tin cup. Or, maybe this man was like you and me, assuming he could deal with his own weaknesses through his own means.

Regardless, it sounds as if the man had resigned himself to his lot in life. We can guess that he may have always hoped for a miracle. Maybe he'd even heard rumors about a miracle-worker from Galilee. But it's likely that he figured his entire life would be spent in darkness. It's easy to give up on hope when your weakness has defined you for so long.

All through my life, people have stopped me in stores, coffee shops, and wherever to pray for God to heal me. I have prayed this prayer by myself, and I have allowed this prayer to be prayed over me. I know 100 percent that God can heal me. When he does, the work of God will be displayed.

But what about *before* he does? Is the work of God still displayed in my life, even if he doesn't heal me today, or tomorrow, or during this lifetime?

The question, then, is this: What do I do with my disability *today*? What should *you* do with your existing weaknesses *today*?

Are we forced to wait in weakness? I say, "Never!" When your daily weaknesses become your daily strengths, you no longer live to wait another day; you live for God to show his power in you *today* and *every day*.

Who are we to limit how "the works of God might be displayed" *today*?

Maybe the man born blind had no idea what was happening until Jesus "spat on the ground, and made clay of the spittle, and applied the clay to his eyes, and said to him, 'Go, wash in the pool of Siloam'" (John 9:6–7). I love this part, which some readers may miss: Jesus used dirt, the same substance with which he created the first man (Gen. 2:7), to repair the man's eyes. What a way to reveal his deity! In his limited state of being human, Jesus reveals his love and power by reaching for the very material—mud—with which he created humankind!

Maybe Jesus had a flashback at that moment to when God had done the same thing with Adam, making the first human being out of clay. Maybe the Trinity of God the Father, Jesus the Son, and the Holy Spirit had a moment when they once again considered how inherently weak we are, that we are but dust—fragile and fleeting.

But God never forgets how weak we truly are. Yet we forget it all the time—until Jesus changes everything.

In the final scene between Jesus and the man born blind, the healed man acknowledges Jesus as the Son of God and worships him:

> Jesus heard that they had put him out, and finding him, He said, "Do you believe in the Son of Man?" He answered, "Who is He, Lord, that I may believe in Him?" Jesus said to him, "You have both seen Him, and He is the one who is talking with you." And he said, "Lord, I believe." And he worshiped him. And Jesus said, "For judgment I came into this world, so that those who do not see may see, and that those who see may become blind." Those of the Pharisees who were with Him heard these things, and said to Him, "We are not blind too, are we?" Jesus said to them, "If you were blind, you

would have no sin; but since you say, 'We see,' your sin remains." (John 9:35–41)

These last three lines amaze me. In so many words, the Pharisees ask Jesus, "Do you think we're weak, like the man born blind?" Jesus replies, "Yep, but you pretend so hard to be strong that you don't even know how weak you really are."

Jesus bends close to the weak. The strong rebuff his patient questioning of their strength. In their arrogance or naivete, they simply don't feel the need for God. In their strength, they fully (and errantly) believe they can do life on their own. But if we were made by God to be in relationship with God, doing life on our own isn't really living. It's just existence.

A life spent wallowing in weakness is a life made small in a prison of its own making. Without outside help, we will never be released.

We're not strong enough to free ourselves.

CHAPTER 2

IMPRISONED BY WEAKNESS

"For we do not have a high priest who cannot sympathize with our weaknesses . . . . Therefore let us draw near with confidence to the throne of grace, so that we may receive mercy and find grace to help in time of need."

—Hebrews 4:15–16

I'm four years old and I've been locked in the bathroom—again.

I don't have a cane, a walker, or a wheelchair. It's just me and my barely functioning legs scrambling to stand up so I can somehow escape.

After wiping away the tears, I stretch my hand toward the doorknob. I think about jumping to reach it, but my body doesn't cooperate with my mind.

I reach again. It's too high. I sit back down on the cold laminate floor in the cramped bathroom that I've become far too familiar with. I'm frustrated, confused, and sad.

Why does he always do this to me? What did I do to deserve this?

Abused

Not only was I born into a weakness I can't control, but I was also born into a household with an abusive dad. In addition to physically and mentally abusing my mother, my father would often lash out at me by trapping me in the bathroom as punishment. I never understood why.

To this day, all I can guess is that maybe my disability was too much for him to handle. Maybe he was abused as a kid. (Hurt people hurt people, right?) Maybe my biological father's weaknesses had been exploited by someone who had supposedly loved him as well.

As an adult remembering that child trapped in a bathroom for no apparent reason, I didn't realize how that abuse had become a deep-seated part of my identity. That ongoing exploitation of my weakness was the first wall of my inner prison. This abuse confined my life and caused me always to feel entrapped by my weakness.

My identity became the boy imprisoned by his disability.

I'm Sorry

I'm thirty years old, and I roll by a laundromat at 11 p.m. A sign in the window reads, "Sorry, we're closed." Like Mitch Hedberg, I comedically think, *Why are you sorry? It's eleven at night! You should be closed!*

However, I could have worn a similar sign around my chest for my entire life: "Sorry, I'm weak."

For the longest time, I apologized for *everything.*

I said I'm sorry for all types of situations outside my control. And, let's face it, considering my disability, I may have more problems than most that are legitimately outside of my control. I repeated that phrase for circumstances that weren't even my fault.

I was an addict. My addiction was saying "I'm sorry." I thought that was my identity until I met Jesus and realized why

I felt the need to apologize so frequently. Even though I was an adult, I was still the little boy trapped by my weakness, imprisoned in the bathroom, crying out, "I'm sorry! I'm sorry! I'm sorry!" for unknown offenses—except for being trapped in a palsied body I thought was to blame for everything.

I was sorry for everything caused by my weakness. I was sorry for having cerebral palsy. I was sorry for getting around slowly in a wheelchair. I was sorry for people having to wait on my slow speech to finally figure out what I was saying. I was sorry for who I was. I was sorry for existing.

Imprisonment by weakness causes an illusion that the weakness is to blame for everything. The weakness becomes the major part of who you are. My weakness defined my life.

> Imprisonment by weakness causes an illusion that your weakness is to blame for everything. The weakness becomes the major part of who you are.

Identity Is Everything

It wasn't until after I'd received my master's degree in seminary that I saw how much my identity had been scarred by my early abuse. As an adult still suffering from an imprisoned mind-set, there were so many doorknobs I thought were still out of my reach:

- I'd always had a desire to live life with a wife and have kids, but my unhealed, insecure heart would run away at the first sign of a woman showing interest in me, a weak inmate.
- Door after door seemed jammed when I began pursuing full-time ministry work, even with my master's degree, excellent references, and years of noteworthy vocational experience.

- When any person showed me love or affection, I didn't trust them out of fear that my weaknesses would again be exploited for their own needs or desires.
- I felt imprisoned by the body I was born with.

Always saying "I'm sorry" to my father led me to believe I needed to apologize to everyone about everything. That's why I was sorry for getting in their way, messing up their plans, and trying to be who God had made me to be.

The problem was that I thought God had made me to be a nuisance with a disability. (Do you ever feel like your weaknesses bother the people in your life?) As a child and teenager, I didn't understand that God had made me to be so much more and that my failure to understand myself was a failure to know who really had the authority to define me.

Thankfully, it wasn't my dad.

Discovering My True Identity

Identity is not just one aspect of being a Christian, it's the *whole* foundation! Who you are—your perspective of yourself—is *everything*. This is explicitly stated by Solomon, the wisest man who ever lived: "For as he thinks within himself, so he is" (Prov. 23:7). I thought I was imprisoned, trapped, worthless, and defined by my disability, and I was sorry for it all.

But after I started having daily quiet times with Jesus in God's Word, my dark instinct of abusing my own identity began to transform. My identity did not need to be founded upon the weaknesses I was born into. I didn't have to be the disabled kid, the abused kid, the confused kid, the different kid, the weak kid, or the kid in a wheelchair with a speech impediment.

While those were parts of my identity, they weren't the *foundation* of my identity. Rather, my daily quiet times with Jesus revealed to me that my identity was in Christ and would always be in Christ. In other words, I needed to stop looking in the mirror and start looking toward God—always. Who I am was not scrawled on the walls of my weakness.

When the truth of my identity permeated my heart and mind, I wrote these life-changing words in my journal as a way to constantly remind myself of who I really am: "Life is more about who Christ is rather than who I am, because who I am is in Christ and Christ in me." I am not defined anymore by myself nor my limitation, but by Christ and him alone!

In his *Confessions*, Augustine of Hippo wrote, "Thou hast made us for thyself, O Lord, and our heart is restless until it finds its rest in thee." If I may be so bold as to edit Augustine, I'd also proclaim that "Thou hast made us for thyself, O Lord, and our identity is unfound and mistaken until it finds itself in thee."

We can never be whole as humans until we allow God to enter into our deepest weaknesses. And we all have so many entrances to let God through.

> "Life is more about who Christ is rather than who I am because who I am is in Christ and Christ in me."

Strength in the Weakness Trap

I'm twelve years old and trapped again, but this time I'm in a hospital. More technically, I'm in an institution for those with cerebral palsy. I'm not physically trapped, but I feel imprisoned.

I've just undergone the first of two major orthopedic surgeries to help bring strength to my legs. I've been told that the post-operational rehabilitation will be demanding. I think, *Why can't the surgery just be enough? Why does it always have to be so hard for me?*

I feel trapped because I'm certain I'm the only kid here who's not mentally disabled. Maybe I should feel bad for those kids, but I'm still a kid myself, so I mostly only feel bad for myself. It's so lonely. I can't really talk with anyone. The surgery was hard. The new metal braces that run from my waist to my toes are all-encompassing. And the ancient metal lock at my knees, to train my legs to walk straight, are unbearable. They feel like a torture chamber.

I'm *not* looking forward to rehab. And I'm supposed to be here for *months*.

What is this? A prison sentence?

Coincidentally enough, at this time in my life, God led me to words written by a man who was stuck in a literal prison yet could still write, "I can do all things through Him who strengthens me" (Phil. 4:13). For painfully obvious reasons, that was my theme verse as a boy. I clung to that verse as tightly as I clung to the bars that were supposed to help me walk at rehab. Only one of those supports never let me down. My newfound strength in Jesus gave me the confidence to face the hourly and daily obstacles my weak body needed to hurdle.

With every challenge that came my way, my mind would chant like *The Little Engine That Could*: "I think I can. I think I can." But, as a kid, I knew that I wasn't an engine being powered by an inanimate object. I "ran" on something—Someone—very different. His Name was Christ. And in my story, he has a role and a function: he's my literal Savior who not only gives me my true identity but now also gives me strength! He is the One I'm going to do *all* things through! Because of the strength he freely gives to weak humans like me, I no longer think I can; I *can*!

Enduring through post-op in that physical, prison-like institution showed me how to survive while still being imprisoned by my weaknesses. I realized I could not only "get along" in life despite what most people saw as major setbacks, but in my weakness, I could do *all* things in life through Christ who gives me strength! I was not only a survivor of a deep weakness, but now, through Christ, I was on the journey to thrive—even in my intense weaknesses.

The Weakness Institution

Years later, I saw how my thinking back then was a result of an institutionalized mind-set. When you've lived with a particular weakness for so long that it becomes normalized—you think you'll always be "that way" because you've always been "that way"—you begin to wonder if your life will ever change for the better. That's an institutionalized mind-set.

Like my cerebral palsy, a weakness couched in an institutional mind-set becomes a jail. Your weakness becomes like invisible prison bars, always preventing you from exploring the full freedoms of your life. The longer you stay trapped behind those bars, the more you resign yourself to believing, *That's just the way things are.* Worse, you may begin to believe, *That's just the way God made me.* All of us must deal with this institution of weakness.

God *did* make you, but we were all born into a fallen, corrupt, sin-infested world. Called "the Fall" after Adam and Eve's fall from God's will in the garden of Eden, this inherited, less-than-ideal spiritual state infects every part of the human condition. In the Fall, we disconnected from the true source of power and began relying on our own strength, which is weakness compared to God's power.

So now we wait in weakness: "We know that the whole creation has been groaning as in the pains of childbirth right up to the present time. Not only so, but we ourselves, who have the firstfruits of the Spirit, groan inwardly as we wait eagerly for our adoption to sonship, the redemption of our bodies" (Rom. 8:22–23 NIV). No one escapes this institution of weakness.

Your weakness might be a chronic disease that leaves you riddled with constant pain. Or it may be a family relationship that went bad decades ago but still gnaws at your heart. Maybe you lost a loved one and still rail at God for the injustice of it. Or maybe you think you lack what is needed to go forward in your career. Maybe you're also weakened physically and it feels all-encompassing. The prison of weakness seems lonely, but everyone has been in that cell—even Jesus.

> When you're freed from the imprisonment of weakness, your weaknesses become a way to praise God and bless others.

But the good news is that hope awaits. Not only does this hope await in the redemption of our weaknesses after we die, but hope awaits even now! What you perceive as a weakness holding you back can be redeemed by God. When you're freed from the imprisonment of weakness, your weaknesses become a way to praise God and bless others. Christ gives you strength that releases you into the world to reveal to others who Jesus is.

After all, he frees his children from prisons of all kinds all the time.

Jesus the Inmate

Jesus doesn't free us from the prison of ourselves from the outside in; he works from the inside out. In other words, he doesn't necessarily change our circumstances. He doesn't change how people around us behave. He doesn't change the consequences of our actions. Rather, he changes our *hearts*. He does so by taking up residence in our prisons.

Let me repeat the verse that opened this chapter—you must know, feel, and understand these truths to see what a friend we truly have in Jesus: "For we do not have a high priest who cannot sympathize with our weaknesses, but One who has been tempted in all things as we are, yet without sin. Therefore let us draw near with confidence to the throne of grace, so that we may receive mercy and find grace to help in time of need" (Heb. 4:15–16).

Have you ever considered that one reason God might have become human was to better empathize with our humanness? God subjected himself to weakness to understand our limitations—to be with us in the jail cell of life.

Jesus sympathizes with our weaknesses. He is incapable of being unsympathetic.

To someone who had felt trapped by so much for so long, these words did for me what I could never do for myself. On my behalf, Jesus reached up and unlocked that unreachable prison lock. An ignorer of weakness is ignoring who you are and the victory you are created to experience in life. A struggle with weakness leads to being an overcomer.

In the prisons of my youth, I couldn't tie my shoes, yet I wanted full independence. My mind moved a mile a minute, but my words failed to keep up. I was known at school, but friendships never seemed to follow me home. I could suffer my father's abuse, but I couldn't stop him from hurting me or anyone else. I apologized to everyone, but I was never really sure why. My prison was that I possessed a gift of vision and envisioned a life I did not have the strength to live.

In focusing on my weaknesses, I'd become depressed. All I could see were the jail bars holding me back. Then something changed. Instead of telling my friends how low I was, I began telling Jesus. I thought, *He's been here! He's experienced that!* I felt his sympathy for my weaknesses—even the big one: cerebral palsy.

I began to trust Jesus with my deepest weaknesses and became transparent and vulnerable with him.

He already knew my hurt and my struggle. Knowing he sympathizes with us in our weaknesses, I discovered he longs for us to come to him so that we may likewise know our hurts and seek the only true healing that will ever soothe our souls. "The Wounded Healer," a lovely title for Jesus coined by theologian Henri Nouwen, began to free me from the prison of my weaknesses and the institution I had created to live in. The all-powerful creator of the universe willingly became encapsulated by weak flesh so that we could have the opportunity to experience a relationship with him.

When Jesus enters your weakness, you feel his sympathy. God has been there, done that. He stepped off the throne to know what it's like to be in your shoes, to live in your prison of weakness. He died and rose to give you all the confidence you need to live in his unmerited favor in your life. At the cross, he became weak to bust you out—to free you from the shackles of weakness.

Because he knew we could never save ourselves, "He Himself bore our sins in His body on the cross, so that we might die to sin and live to righteousness; for by His wounds you were healed" (1 Pet. 2:24). And it's fascinating and shocking and mysterious that our redemption required what's so inevitable in this life: weakness. God let himself experience one of the deepest forms of fleshly weakness—physical wounds—to redeem and heal us.

As he died for us, so too must we die to self and die for others. Jesus invites you into the resurrected life by unlocking the tomb of weakness.

Glowing Hope in the Struggle

I'm six years old and can't believe what I'm seeing. I'm asleep, but I feel like I've never been more awake. My young mind wants to believe I'm seeing an angel in this dream, but even as a child, I fight that notion. *Angels are just in Bible stories, right?*

But this experience was real. It was not just a dream, but a trance. The angelic creature approaches me as I'm still lying in bed. I feel a little fear, but mostly I feel joy and comfort. But he doesn't stop at my bed. Rather, he goes to the corner of the room where my cane is propped against a wall. He grabs that cane and replaces it with one that glows.

Somehow, I comprehend—or maybe the adult me looking back understands—that this new cane represents my calling to bring comfort to others. The glowing cane brought me supernatural comfort, and I realized that God desired that comfort to overflow through my life and into other's lives. The glowing cane was 2 Corinthians 1:4 becoming real in my life: "[God] comforts us in all our affliction so that we will be able to comfort those who are in any affliction with the comfort with which we ourselves are comforted by God." With God's help, he'll use my weakness to help people. He will take what I'd always seen as a negative and turn it into a positive. Weakness is one place God's purposes dwell and can be used to show his purposes to others.

I often wonder if other people imagine I'm mad at God for not healing me yet. I also wonder if those with chronic illnesses, or prayer requests they've been praying about for decades without a seeming answer, get upset with God because he doesn't heal them or answer their prayers in the way they want or on the timeline they desire. But God is not to blame for our weakness.

> Weakness is one place God's purposes dwell and can be used to show his purposes to others.

Jesus unlocks the unreachable doorknob to the institution, the prison in which your weaknesses have trapped you. When you struggle in weakness, he won't let you endure it alone. He'll provide himself or an angel to comfort you. In other words, he'll enter into your prison with you—and break you free.

Until that healing happens, his purposes still prevail.

These are the times and places where we learn and experience that Jesus is enough. Grace is enough for every situation and for each one of our weaknesses. We lean into Jesus when we feel overwhelmed by our weakness. We speak to Jesus like we would a most trusted friend who we know always has our best interests at heart. We may whine, complain, and bemoan our life, but Jesus, the Great Sympathizer and the Wounded Healer, patiently, lovingly, dotingly listens.

God was with me when I was locked in the bathroom. God was with me in my weakness when I felt imprisoned in that CP institution. He was with me when I felt locked and chained to a wheelchair. And he *is* with me every day; not despite my weaknesses, but right within them.

He wants to rescue you from Satan's dark realm where weakness imprisons, too. He wants to save you into Jesus's kingdom, where he redeems and sympathizes with you in all of your weakness: "For he has rescued us from the kingdom of darkness and transferred us into the Kingdom of his dear Son" (Col. 1:13 NLT).

What we all secretly and desperately want is what God not-so-secretly but oh-so-desperately wants to give to us in our time of need: grace, the unmerited favor of God. This grace can't be earned or deserved, and neither can our weaknesses make God turn his face away from us. The good news is that grace is a gift during times of need in our weakness. God wants these black-and-white words to become living color in our lives just like they did for a long-named guy in the Old Testament: Mephibosheth.

"That I May Show Him Kindness"

Mephibosheth's story isn't one that's often taught in Sunday school classes, but it should be. Requiring just thirteen verses in 2 Samuel 9:1–13, this child's story is a quick yet fantastic glimpse into the way God works and the way he desires us to receive grace: unmerited favor in our weakness.

Mephibosheth is Jonathan's son and Saul's grandson. Saul was the king of Israel prior to King David. And David and Jonathan were such good friends that the Bible says, "the soul of Jonathan was knit to the soul of David" (1 Sam. 18:1). Immediately prior to David's reign, Saul and Jonathan died during a battle with the Philistines. Once David becomes king, he asks his court, "Is there yet anyone left of the house of Saul, that I may show him kindness for Jonathan's sake?" (2 Sam. 9:1).

Of course, you know who's left: Mephibosheth.

The other reason I like this story so much is what we're then told about the boy: he is "a son of Jonathan who is crippled in both feet" (2 Sam. 9:3). Mephibosheth could be me, just a few centuries removed—but maybe with a descriptor a little more politically correct, like "physically challenged."

When Mephibosheth enters David's court, something fascinating happens that most people may read right over: Mephibosheth "fell on his face and prostrated himself. And David said, 'Mephibosheth.' And he said, 'Here is your servant!' David said to him, 'Do not fear'" (2 Sam. 9:6–7a). Why is Mephibosheth afraid of David? Because common ancient practice was to kill every member of a former ruling class so any remaining family members couldn't usurp the throne. Mephibosheth feared for his life.

But David, "a man after [God's] heart" (Acts 13:22), doesn't bestow death; he breathes life: "Do not fear, for I will surely show kindness to you for the sake of your father Jonathan, and will restore to you all the land of your grandfather Saul; and you shall eat at my table regularly" (2 Sam. 9:7). Instead of being killed on the spot, Mephibosheth receives his rightful inheritance. But David's grace goes even further, as grace always does: "Mephibosheth ate at David's table as one of the king's sons" (2 Sam. 9:11b). David effectively adopts Mephibosheth, the young physically challenged grandson of a former king who often wanted to kill David.

This is the good news of the gospel foreshadowed in an Old Testament story. We're all Mephibosheth: weak and afraid. But grace, the unmerited favor of God, awaits us all when we can just say, "Here is your servant!" (2 Sam. 9:6). And the reality of belief in Christ not only means that we won't be put to death, but that we'll be granted our inheritance in Christ. And not only that, but we'll be adopted as sons and daughters of the king. "The Spirit Himself testifies with our spirit that we are children of God, and if children, heirs also, heirs of God and fellow heirs with Christ, if indeed we suffer with Him so that we may also be glorified with Him" (Rom. 8:16–17).

> Struggling through your weakness is a huge step toward walking in the true identity of who you are in Christ.

Grace is God's abundant kindness shown to us in the depths of our weakness. Let's receive his unmerited favor in our weaknesses.

In my weaknesses, after God broke me free from the imprisonment of weakness, I now thrive in who I am in Christ, I can do all things through him, and his unmerited favor is always available to me. This is how you struggle well in weakness. Struggling through your weakness is a huge step toward walking in the true identity of who you are in Christ.

Knowing God subjected himself to weakness by becoming human and suffering on the cross reminds me that I'm not alone in my weakness. That's how you will come to see that your weaknesses are meant to be redefined by the only One worthy enough to define you: Jesus.

CHAPTER 3

WEAKNESS REDEFINED

"And He has said to me, 'My grace is sufficient for you, for power is perfected in weakness.'"
—2 Corinthians 12:9a

"You talk funny!"

Willie was ten, and he was laughing at me. I'm pretty sure he'd never met anyone like me. I responded to his laughter with a hug. I was trying to serve his family in St. Louis on a one-week mission trip a few months after graduating from college. It was the first of many travel adventures I'd always anticipated going on.

Willie was Mary's grandson. He was also one of eighteen people living in Mary's two-bedroom transient home. And I thought my family's four-bedroom home with a few siblings was cramped back home.

Their house wasn't just small and overcrowded. It had become so dilapidated that I feared just rolling around inside would cause it to crash to the ground—as if I were a bowling ball and the house was filled with pins.

Their neighborhood reminded me of pictures and news reports I'd seen of developing countries. I'd never seen such poverty up close. This inner-city St. Louis neighborhood was the poorest place I'd ever experienced.

While there, so much was stirred within me. My heart broke for its residents. At the same time, anxiety about overcoming my own physical obstacles on this trip gave way to empathy for their daily lives.

To get to their house, our team had to weave through streets due to barricades blocking different entrances to their neighborhood. I couldn't figure out why the barricades were there until I asked someone.

"Drive-by shootings."

"You're . . . kidding me."

For the first time in my life, I witnessed a different kind of weakness. Like the imprisonment and struggles I've faced, I saw weakness covering the whole neighborhood. For another first, I had an opportunity to meet others right where they were: imprisoned by weakness.

I had no idea that actual walls had to be used to block the way from drive-by shootings. The danger of my surroundings became real. My lack of strength to protect myself—or anyone else—became real. The fears I'd had before coming on this mission trip jumped into my throat. In my mind, we really were rolling into the belly of the beast, and every weakness that made me who I was seemed easy for the beast to conquer.

I looked around to make sure no cars were driving by, then I bowled myself into their house.

In the dim light, I couldn't see how anyone, let alone eighteen people, could live in such a house. The sick-sweet smell of sewer water emanated from their uninhabitable basement. As I rolled past the bathroom, I saw sleeping bags (and more standing water). With a shock, I realized that the house had so little room that at least a few people had to sleep in the bathroom.

Along with the unique smells of the house, the realities of their situation and mine began to sink in to me. This was going to be a much more challenging trip than I'd thought—but not in the way I thought it would challenge me.

In fact, prior to leaving, I was more concerned about myself. *How am I going to get anywhere? What's the accessibility like in an inner-city area? How will I relate to people I don't know who are so different from me? After all, I'm supposedly going there to help them. What if something bad happens while we're there? Isn't St. Louis one of the most dangerous cities in the world? How is a guy in a wheelchair going to hit the deck if a drive-by happens?*

I was worrying about my weaknesses more than I was trusting in God. My limitations and weaknesses were compounded by the weaknesses and limitations around me. For all my life, I had dealt with weaknesses in a surviving mind-set. I had never anticipated, especially in those circumstances, that I was about to embark on a thriving life.

Even in my weakness of worrying, God would ultimately use this trip to forever alter my life.

Seeing People and Myself in a New Way

I'll never forget their welcoming routine. Starting on just my second visit to Mary's house, once they'd gotten to know me and little Willie would walk up to me to receive big hugs, I'd drive up to their house, honk my horn, and they'd all instantly appear near my car.

They seemed so excited to welcome me and hear more about Jesus that they wouldn't let me get my wheelchair out of my car. They'd get it for me, and then they'd walk on each side of me as we went into their home. They seemed to long to hear how Jesus helped me in my weaknesses.

But this family, who was encouraged by me living life through Christ who gives me strength, actually encouraged *me* through that powerful experience. Their walking with me was a visual reminder that Christ would always be my strength.

I was amazed at how God was actually using my weakness to demolish the wall my mind had erected in front of this family before I'd even met them. It's like I'd placed them behind a mental barricade with the words *inaccessible*, *different*, and *poor* emblazoned on it, all depicting different weaknesses from mine, but, at the same time, they suffered weaknesses all the same. God was giving me his eyes for them. Apparently, they had the same eyes for me. In all this, God was giving me new eyes for myself.

I thought about how God can change our perspective about others and ourselves. Most remember David in the Bible as a king, a prayer warrior, and a victor. But this is not how I remember him. This was how people saw him at first. God's will was for David to be king, but Samuel, who had the authority to make David king, saw David, in his small stature, as anything but a king. Then God redeems how Samuel sees David's stature: "But the LORD said to Samuel, 'Do not look at his appearance or at the height of his stature, because I have rejected him; for God sees not as man sees, for man looks at the outward appearance, but the LORD looks at the heart'" (1 Sam. 16:7).

In the midst of loving people in the inner city, Jesus gave me his eyes for my new friends. Not only was God transforming how I see people, but he was also transforming and healing my heart regarding how I'm seen by people and by him. Wow—God sees me, not by my slur of speech and palsied body, but he sees my heart!

I feared I wouldn't be able to get around in the inner city. This family became my legs. I feared that I was too different from them or that they were too different from me. This family treated me like family. I feared that their poorness meant they were hopeless. This family gave me hope.

Minute by minute, I saw God transforming every weakness that had plagued my mind into a strength. And as I began to see myself in just as much need of Christ as they were, God revealed a wonderful (and wonderfully humbling) truth to me: although in very different ways, we were all minorities. We all had particular challenges to overcome. We all needed Christ to be our strength, especially when the world around us judged us based on appearances.

I was this family. This family was me. And Christ was in all.

Strong John Choosing to Decrease

In the midst of finding new perspectives, I met a new friend in St. Louis as well. John is a charismatic leader. All who meet him are able to tell that upon their first encounter with him. His mannerisms, appearance, and demeanor commanded immediate respect. Whatever room John is in, his countenance draws people to him.

It seemed like every kid in the neighborhood wanted to be like John. They dressed like him, and they longed to be in his gang—whatever gang he was about to choose. Every gang wanted John, including the two main gangs in the city. John was about to choose which one to join, but then John met me. He exuded strength, and in a tough neighborhood that has to use barricades because of drive-bys, this strength seemed unrivaled.

So, to see Strong John next to Weak Todd was an oddity. We were night and day in so many ways. And yet we shared one significant characteristic: we both believed in Jesus. In fact, John had just given his life to Christ a few weeks before my arrival in St. Louis. When I first spoke to him and told him about why I was in town, he told me that he'd been looking for someone to disciple him. He desired to know what a real leader in the kingdom of God looks like—and he was looking to me for that example.

I thought, *How ironic that this epitome of strength sees leadership material in a stuttering, palsied man like me.* I was honored and dumbfounded at the same time.

John was hungry to learn what it means to walk in Jesus's power and strength. I could tell his heart had been changed, because he spoke about how he knew his own strength was just a facade—that it was earthly power. He desired to walk in the power of dying to self and living in the life of Jesus. He was admitting and professing his own weaknesses.

I thought, *How ironic that I'm learning the same lessons as John: the semantics we use for "strength" and "weakness" do not mean the same in God's language in his kingdom.*

John reminded me of another John. Like ex-gangster John, John the Baptist had a rough outer appearance: "Now John himself had a garment of camel's hair and a leather belt around his waist; and his food was locusts and wild honey" (Matt. 3:4). Both Johns didn't care what the people of the world thought of them according to their outer appearance and status on the streets. They both grasped their God-given callings deep in their hearts: to prepare the way for the Lord. Ex-gangster John prepared the way in his own heart. John the Baptist prepared people's hearts for Jesus: "Behold, I send My messenger ahead of You, Who will prepare Your way; The voice of one crying in the wilderness, 'Make ready the way of the Lord, Make His paths straight'" (Mark 1:2–3).

Yet there is a characteristic of both of these Johns that prepared the way in *my* heart for God to give me a fresh perspective of myself and to set me up for my lifelong calling. Ex-gangster John lived it. John the Baptist powerfully yet simply proclaimed, "He must increase, but I must decrease" (John 3:30). Both Johns decreased in status. Jesus increased in them and through them.

"More of Jesus; less of myself." These words amplified in my heart and in my mind as I was thinking less of my weaknesses and more of Jesus.

My new friend John, who was a very important person among many who looked up to him on the dangerous streets of St. Louis, was purposefully making himself less important. Another version of the Bible translates John the Baptist's impacting words this way: "He must become more important. I must become less important" (John 3:30 NLV). Both of these men exemplify to me what's important in life. It's about how big, awesome, important, powerful, and strong God is rather than how weak, disfluent, slow, and palsied I am.

Displaying the splendor of God—how great he is—is the point of life. The way I define life through my weakness is not the point. Life is more about who Christ is rather than who I am, because I am in Christ and Christ is in me. Life is more about what God can do rather than what I am able—or not able—to do, and I get to join the all-powerful God in what he is doing!

I didn't realize it at that moment, but God was using John to kick-start my calling to show strength to the weak by boasting in my weaknesses as strengths. And not that I'd ever think to compare myself to the Old Testament saints like Abraham, Moses, and Gideon, but now I know that God was patiently raising me up just like he did those men: by showing me time and again that the facade of self-reliance (aka, focusing on weakness) only hides our deep need for reliance on God.

This reliance is derived from a deep understanding of who God is in all his might, and knowing that life is more worthwhile when we

> Life is more about who Christ is rather than who I am, because I am in Christ and Christ is in me.

die not only to relying on ourselves but also to compensating for our weaknesses. For most of my life, my weaknesses were my focal point, my center stage, the single factor that kept me from fulfilling the dreams and desires of my heart. These weaknesses became the focus of my identity.

The two Johns gave me the gift of a mind shift that changed the rest of my life! Jesus Christ, his power, and what he can do became my center stage. And this all happened on the streets of St. Louis, where I'd never before felt so weak.

Basking in God's Presence

In spending so much focused time serving in St. Louis, I began to understand a central fact of the Christian life: following Jesus and setting him at center stage is all about moments. Jesus-centered living is time spent with others for the express purpose of sharing and showing Christ's love to them. Quiet time with Jesus is key to loving others. Intimacy with Jesus through daily quiet times overflows into loving people around you.

Following Jesus is just allowing Jesus to meet another person through you. Intimacy and overflow are how this occurs. Quiet times with Jesus empower me to love people where they are, just like God loves me right where I am on that very day. But I never expected, during just another quiet time in St. Louis, that God would deeply speak into me in a way that would completely alter my life. He met me exactly where I was so I could become exactly who he wanted me to be.

The Words That Changed My Life

Sharing God's love and hope to John and to Mary's family—and having my heart touched by them—was a breakthrough moment for me. For the first time, I thought and believed *weak* is *the new strong.* I was grasping that what I'd always viewed as a deficiency, God viewed as his sufficiency.

Then, during a regular daily quiet time on that trip at a café in St. Louis, God's Holy Spirit led me to words in the Bible that would radically change my life and my perspective of who I am forever. In 2 Corinthians, I saw a theme forming that so closely aligned with what I'd experienced that week that I couldn't help but know God was behind the scenes of it all and about to become center stage in what seemed to be the largest weakness of my life. What I read corresponded too closely to where I was in my spiritual walk. Paul shares:

> For this reason, to keep me from exalting myself, there was given me a thorn in the flesh, a messenger of Satan to torment me—to keep me from exalting myself! Concerning this I implored the Lord three times that it might leave me. And He has said to me, "My grace is sufficient for you, for power is perfected in weakness." Most gladly, therefore, I will rather boast about my weaknesses, so that the power of Christ may dwell in me. Therefore I am well content with weaknesses, with insults, with distresses, with persecutions, with difficulties, for Christ's sake; for when I am weak, then I am strong. (2 Cor. 12:7b–10 NASB)

When I read God's answer to Paul's pleas, "My grace is sufficient for you, for power is perfected in weakness," the ground beneath my wheelchair felt like it shook. I'm sure it didn't, because I was in St. Louis, where earthquakes are uncommon and low magnitude, but my world *had* just been rocked.

I wept.

"My grace is sufficient for you, for power is perfected in weakness" became my life motto. I wept with joy upon reading it and understanding its truth. At that moment, God revealed my purpose to me: to boast in my insufficiency so that God might always be seen as sufficient.

Despite the other people in that café on that morning, I shouted, "THANK YOU, JESUS!"

With tears of joy rolling down my face and new revelations of grace impacting my heart, I proclaimed, "Jesus, your unmerited favor is all I need! Thank you for your power made perfect through my weakness: cerebral palsy! Thank you for the joy in being weak! Thank you for your power that dwells in me! I'm blessed! I'm content! If all of this can display your power and glory, then praise your name! Weak is the new strong! Amen!"

They probably gave me weird stares, but I don't really know. I didn't care at that moment. All I knew is that I'd been freed from the burdens I carried with me into St. Louis from the time I was born. I knew I'd be going home different, lighter—still weak, yet stronger. Since that transformative moment, I've studied, pondered, and prayed over this passage many times. God is faithful to focus my heart and mind on something different each time, something that speaks to exactly where I am and what I need.

We have a choice. We can let our weaknesses define us—the message that Satan wants us to embrace. Or we can live in the truth that our weaknesses are the conduit God uses to display his power.

The thorn in the flesh, a tormenting messenger of Satan, was Paul's weakness. Accusations from the Evil One are nothing new. In fact, Satan is after us; and one way he assaults us is through attacking our identity in Christ. Satan would love to accuse us and for us to receive his message that our weaknesses define us. The good news is that Satan was defeated at the cross, where God became his weakest. Jesus defeated Satan in our lives where we're the weakest.

We no longer have to listen to Satan and how he torments us by defining lies. Now there's a louder voice: "Then I heard a loud voice in heaven, saying, 'Now the salvation, and the power, and the kingdom of our God and the authority of His Christ have come, for *the accuser of our brethren has been thrown down*, he who accuses them before our God day and night. And *they overcame him because of the blood of the Lamb* and because of the word of their testimony, and they did not love their life even when faced with death'" (Rev. 12:10–11—emphasis mine).

The Bible is the good news of Jesus, and your testimony—your story—is the gospel in living color. God gave me my testimony in that café. He gave me victory over Satan and his lies that had caused me to identify my life by my weakness. I realized all my weaknesses are a conduit for God to perfect and display his power! In the same body in which I was defeated, now I have the victory!

The fuel, as we see in this weakness-redeeming Scripture, that ignites God's power in our weaknesses is grace, the unmerited favor of God. Grace is God willingly applying his ability and power through us to accomplish his will on earth as it is in heaven. Grace is God empowering us to accomplish the things in life that we cannot accomplish in our own strength. Grace makes way for the power of God to be placed in us that enables us to live a victorious life! With our own strength and abilities, we can sometimes do the possible, but God's grace empowers us to do the impossible. Truly, it seems God always calls us to do the impossible; but with his grace working in our lives, the impossible becomes a reality.

> The Bible is the good news of Jesus, and your testimony—your story—is the gospel in living color.

Even though we don't deserve his great and awesome power, he gives us his power as a free gift of unmerited favor. In order for us to be able to accomplish the will of God, we must tap into his grace. There's no limit to God's grace. It's boundless! There's no limit to his power either. Believe that the impossible is possible with him and his power displayed through you!

God's power is perfected in our weakness. That's an astounding phrase. A perfect God allows his perfection to be made real within us? That ought to blow us away! God willingly chooses to work in the lives of the weak so that his perfect power might be seen and experienced in a fallen world. In fact, some Bible translations use the word "displayed" instead of "made," further indicating that all who rely on God ultimately reveal his power not despite their weaknesses, but within them.

As for "I will rather boast about my weaknesses," this book is my boasting! Where I was once ashamed of my legs, my speech disfluency, and my wheelchair, now I'm glad God chose me to bear witness to his power through my life. And can you imagine what the world would be like if we all boasted in our weaknesses? To stop pretending that everything's always okay? To let our guards down, take our masks off, and stop lying to each other that we're strong when we're actually just barely hanging on? Once we boast in weakness, we'll experience the second part of that verse: "So that the power of Christ may dwell in me." We have access to the all-surpassing power that created the heavens and the earth—and that power is within *you*!

Lastly, I've learned to be "well content with weaknesses" to the point that I *delight* in them. Why? Because understanding my weaknesses, like cerebral palsy, and getting real about their effects on my life help me better see God's power at work. I've always been inspired to practice this truth. Psalm 37:4 charges: "Delight yourself in the LORD; And He will give you the desires of your heart." Part of such "delight" is delighting in my weaknesses. Instead of raising my fists at God, instead of Satan, who is the antagonist, in righteous indignation over the hand I've been dealt, I gratefully accept what's been given to me because I know it can be used to display God's power to a dying world, "for when I am weak, then I am strong." What a privilege to be redefined by this new identity and to be empowered by this to fulfill our calling in life not despite our weaknesses, but by God's power flowing *through* our weaknesses.

Heeding the Call

Over future quiet times, the Bible's themes of strength and weakness popped from every page as if I'd highlighted them. I realized that time and again, God didn't use strong people or perfect people to accomplish his plans. He used the weak. He used the willing. He used the faithful. He used those who knew their weaknesses but knew God could transform their small offerings into something much greater than they could have ever imagined. He used people made of clay: "But we have this treasure in jars of clay to show that this all-surpassing power is from God and not from us" (2 Cor. 4:7 NIV).

Even though I knew my life had a purpose, I didn't know what it specifically was until that day in that St. Louis café. I had a severe physical challenge that had always made me feel different from everyone else. I struggled for so long to understand why God had allowed that to happen to me. When I'd listen to U2's "I Still Haven't Found What I'm Looking For," I'd nod my head in agreement.

But then, I finally understood why God had made me perfectly and Satan had made a failed attempt to thwart God's plans—and I was thankful, even joyful. My wheelchair is a *chariot*. My speech impediment is an unusual *bridge-builder*. My weaknesses are my *strengths*. What I'd always seen as the thorn in my side was a way to remember that God is sufficient to meet all my needs. (2 Cor. 12:7)

I had prayed so hard and for so long for God to completely heal me. On that day in St. Louis, he did, but not in the way I had imagined my healing. I didn't get up from my wheelchair for the last time. My speech impediment didn't disappear. But I was healed. He healed my perspective and redefined what I see as weakness. He revealed my identity to me: a fully loved son of God whom he could use regardless of how the world perceived me. Yes, God can heal me physically. But for now, my weakness is a blessing to let his power, grace, and unmerited favor be known to each person I meet.

In a flash, God caused me to think about my past. I saw why so many students had been drawn to me throughout my school years. Even though it was obvious I didn't play football, jocks befriended me. Even though I never smoked anything, stoners wafted over to me. Even though my speech would extend a cheer into a day-long event, cheerleaders rallied around me. All kinds of nerds, preppies, and popular kids sought to become my friends.

I saw that they hadn't necessarily been drawn to me, but they'd been drawn to God's power within me. Despite my external appearance and stuttering ways, I had a supernatural confidence in God that was appealing. I didn't understand that in high school and college, but God shed light on those experiences during that St. Louis quiet time. I realized we ought to take our deepest insecurities and weaknesses to Jesus and let him redeem them to display his power through them.

Can you tell that I have a soft spot in my heart for St. Louis?

After that one-week trip ended, I wept with compassion for the people without Jesus's love and power in inner-city St. Louis. I had a better understanding of what it meant to truly live in poverty. But I also had a better understanding of how the light of hope can break into any person's life who will receive Jesus and his power. In considering my time there and the dozens of people I'd encountered, God called me to become a full-time vocational minister.

He wanted me to reach the weak to show them that their weaknesses, in God's hands, were strengths. He wanted to use this mobile jar of clay to reveal to others God's all-surpassing power, which is only and ever made perfect in weakness. That's when I finally and fully dedicated my life to the ministry of Jesus Christ.

Mom's Prayer and the Rest of My Life

That fall, I began attending seminary at Abilene Christian University. When I told my mom about my decision to go into full-time vocational ministry, she told me something she'd kept secret ever since I was born: "Todd, when you were born, you almost died. I asked God, 'Lord, if you will just let my son live, please, may he be a minister for you!'"

God was in the process of answering that prayer. He had allowed me to live, and now he was setting me on a path to become a minister. In time, I earned a master's in biblical and related studies, which opened doors for me to become the full-time minister he had called me to be.

Sharing the gospel through my life and words has become my greatest passion. I can't help but speak, share, and show the love of Christ every day. That this is my lifelong career amazes me. That God would choose to use someone like me amazes me even more. So I cling to him in gratefulness. I worship him in awe. And I share him with others because what he's done with me, I know he can do with everyone else. You don't have to be a minister to experience God's power in your weakness. You can just be you.

Now, when I think about God's call on my life, I hear Willie's laugh—a reminder that what sets me apart is what God can use.

CHAPTER 4

TRANSPARENT WEAKNESS OPENS DOORS

*"On my own behalf I will not boast,
except in regard to my weaknesses."*
—2 Corinthians 12:5

I'll never forget Dusty, my faith mentor at Louisiana State University. Though he taught me much, I will always remember one particular lesson about weakness that he modeled for me—and that I thought he was ridiculous even to attempt.

I met Dusty on that mission trip to St. Louis that redefined my weakness. He later invited me to consider a position as one of his campus minister interns at LSU. The year after I earned my master's degree, I took him up on the offer. Believing that I wasn't quite ready for a full-fledged ministry position by myself, I was excited to reunite with Dusty and to learn more about what my future vocation could look like. I was insecure about my capabilities to lead an organization by myself. This internship seemed like the perfect fit for my inadequacy. After all, I'd have a guide to show me the ropes—and how to get *through* the ropes.

Quicker than I roll or talk, my expectations were soon to be upended.

On the same day I unpacked at LSU, Dusty told me he'd applied for a job in Colorado.

I was incredulous.

Dusty could tell I was disappointed, so he encouraged me that God could certainly still use me in Baton Rouge and that I wouldn't need his help.

But even thinking about not having Dusty to help me made me all the more overwhelmed. My insecurities seemed to double during the span of that conversation. *How would I ever do what I'm supposed to do in this ministry without Dusty's leadership to guide me?*

To try to take the spotlight off myself, I asked him about the position in Colorado.

Dusty told me about the job, and then he shared a lesson in weakness I'll never forget: "I think you'd appreciate my cover letter, Todd. I didn't list my strengths, my education, or my past ministry experiences that could benefit this new church."

I'm sure my eyes conveyed what I was thinking: *Then what else could you have sent?*

Dusty answered my unspoken question: "I just shared my weaknesses and struggles."

"No way."

"Yes way. Here, let me get it for you."

Dusty found his cover letter and handed it to me. I read it over. Sure enough, the letter was all about Dusty's weaknesses. It was the strangest cover letter I'd ever seen.

My face may have conveyed shock, but I was smiling on the inside. *What kind of church would ever hire someone based on a letter like this? Maybe one will. Maybe it can be a new normal for churches to seek and pursue weak, vulnerable ministers. But I doubt it. If this is what Dusty's going to send off, then what am I worried about? He'll surely be here for this entire year! I won't have to do this by myself after all. No church is going to hire someone based on a resume like this.*

My insecurities instantly disappeared—until a week later, over lunch.

"Todd, I got the job."

Dusty moved two weeks later, and I was left without the main reason I'd taken that internship.

Overlooked Due to Weakness

I don't begrudge Dusty for taking that job. It's just that I was so certain a cover letter like that wouldn't fly in today's culture, corporations, and even Christian organizations. And I was so excited to apprentice under him while at LSU. Not knowing what I was doing and full of insecurities about my aptitude to do the job, I trusted in the God who had redefined my disability. *Do I dare trust him with all my insecurities about the rest of my weaknesses?* God still worked through my immaturity and lack of on-the-job experience. In fact, that's when I received most of my on-the-job experience.

In the weeks and months following Dusty's departure, his cover letter kept coming to mind: *This is the kind of cover letter I'm now writing in my life.* I asked myself, *Can I trust people to read it with an open heart like Dusty's recipients read his letter?*

The church that had hired him obviously didn't see him from a typical, worldly perspective. They must have known their Bibles; they knew that God shows off the most through those who are unashamed to boast in their weaknesses and expose their vulnerabilities. They knew that their church could experience God's power through a transparent leader like Dusty. They knew that hiring a "weak" pastor could likewise allow their church members to acknowledge their own weaknesses—the only real place where Christ can begin to work.

My revelation over Dusty's cover letter became even more real to me as my internship year drew to a close. Now I was the one sending out cover letters. And because I wanted to focus on a particular field still within collegiate ministry, there were only a few job openings at different universities.

Without fail, I was always one of the top three candidates being considered for the job—until the hiring personnel discovered that I had cerebral palsy. As soon as they heard me speak or saw me in person, the hiring process suddenly halted.

Their "discovery" of my CP always amused me too. All of my references said that it was *because* of my physical challenges that I was able to share the gospel with so many. My references had seen and experienced how God consistently used my disability to break down all kinds of barriers. They knew that other people *never* felt intimidated to talk with me. So I had to ask myself: *Had these hiring personnel even talked to my references? Have they read my letter?*

If they had, it was my hope that they'd easily see that one of my major strengths in ministry *is* my CP! Though it may look like weakness from the outside (or from the black-and-white sentences of a cover letter), God works in and through my CP, my wheelchair, and my speech impediment. He doesn't work *despite* my weaknesses; he works *through* them.

Still, I wondered: Was anyone, anywhere ever going to hire someone like me?

Paul Was the Model of Biblical Transparency

While I was getting frustrated at being passed over for job after job, God reminded me that I'd seen a cover letter like Dusty's before, and it was from a much older source.

In the apostle Paul's first letter to the church at Corinth, he was defending his ministry through a cover letter, of sorts, but he was doing so through proclaiming his weaknesses and not the many strengths he could have used to persuade that church. Paul aptly summarized what I daily experience: "God has chosen the foolish things of the world to shame the wise, and God has chosen the weak things of the world to shame the things which are strong" (1 Cor. 1:27).

It's amazing to think that Paul could have used his stature, power, and former experiences to persuade the church to his side in any argument. Paul knew he could make that argument too, as he lays out his "worldly" cover letter to the Philippians: "If anyone else has a mind to put confidence in the flesh, I far more: circumcised the eighth day, of the nation of Israel, of the tribe of Benjamin, a Hebrew of Hebrews; as to the Law, a Pharisee; as to zeal, a persecutor of the church; as to the righteousness which is in the Law, found blameless" (Phil. 3:4–6).

In the eyes of those to whom he was writing, Paul had it all: cultural status, achievement after achievement, a high education, proven religious leadership, unmatched zeal, and a deep desire for holiness. If I were to update Paul's words "to put confidence in the flesh" in a ministerial cover letter today, an exemplary letter might read:

- Christian since before I could read
- Lifelong church service attender
- Two decades of proven ministry experience
- Thousands of conversions
- No scandals
- Married to one wife for twenty-plus years
- Two well-adjusted children

In other words, some cover letters boast in the flesh, but ministers should not only feel free but also encouraged to boast in their weaknesses—just as Paul did, and just as Dusty did.

Through experiencing the power of the risen Lord, Paul knew through and through that all of his worldly accolades were rubbish compared to knowing Christ Jesus. After listing his accomplishments, Paul writes, "But whatever things were gain to me, those things I have counted as loss for the sake of Christ. More than that, I count all things to be loss in view of the surpassing value of knowing Christ Jesus my Lord, for whom I have suffered the loss of all things, and count them but rubbish so that I may gain Christ" (Phil. 3:7–8).

When writing to the Corinthians, another early church who would have been impressed by Paul's resume, he didn't list his strengths. Maybe Dusty wasn't the pioneer of this kind of cover letter after all. Rather, the apostle Paul wrote, "If I have to boast, I will boast of what pertains to my weakness" (2 Cor. 11:30). And just so the Corinthians understand what he's saying, he repeats himself just a few verses later: "On my own behalf I will not boast, except in regard to my weaknesses" (2 Cor.12:5b).

To put this into a modern context, it's like Michael Jordan, when he's up to be voted into the Hall of Fame, telling the NBA to look at his brief and unsuccessful tenure in minor league baseball but not at his long list of basketball accomplishments. It just doesn't make sense! To boast in our weaknesses is *not* how we defend our careers.

We put our best feet forward at all times. (Some of us put our best wheels forward.) We headline our good deeds. We tweet our highlights. We devise our best answers at every job interview.

I'm reminded of what applicants will sometimes answer to that oft-asked question during a job interview: "What's your greatest weakness?"

"Well, my greatest weakness is also my greatest strength." Then they'll go into a convoluted reason why their laziness, tardiness, or workaholism is actually a benefit to the company. They don't want to be seen as having *any* weaknesses, which is ridiculous because we all have weaknesses.

Erecting a false front of strength also brings to mind how people act on a first date. Typically, people want to be seen as the best possible version of themselves, so a guy takes a shower for the first time in a week, throws on clothes that have actually been washed, and holds the door open for his date. A girl is likewise on her best behavior and maybe doesn't eat as much (or at all) and makes a mental note not to talk about her ex at dinner. The couple is well-meaning, but they're not being authentic with each other.

In other words, bragging about our strengths doesn't just happen with words. It happens in the way we present ourselves to others, as well as the words we use to talk about ourselves. Boasting in our strengths happens at home, at work, at school, at . . . well, anywhere we are, because we tend to want to minimize our weaknesses and maximize our strengths so that others will see us in the best light possible. (And, ridiculously, sometimes we think we can get God to believe the same thing about us!)

Truth be told, this *isn't* my default mode. I feel as if I have nothing else *but* my weaknesses in which to brag. To be able to boast about your weakness is *so incredibly freeing.* When you understand that Christ's power can work through any of your weaknesses, you no longer have the fear of being found out as a weak person. And when fear leaves, that's when you can really begin to thrive in your life, your relationships, and your career.

> When fear leaves, that's when you can really begin to thrive in your life, your relationships, and your career.

The fruit of my ministry did not come about despite my CP, but *because* of it. What I mean is that when I chose to boast in my weakness, just as Paul did, and I began to understand that God could use even me *in my current state*, his power through me began changing lives *through* my CP. For example:

- I am not a gifted speaker because I've been granted eloquence. Rather, I believe I'm a gifted speaker because people have to slow down to understand what I'm saying. When people are forced to pay such attention to words (that I always pray are more from God than from me), those words can't help but touch hearts hungry for truth.
- I am not such a happy-go-lucky person all the time that people constantly smile around me. Rather, I believe that some people are encouraged and feel hope by my faith and tenacity. When they see that most actions in my life require ten times the amount of time they'd need to accomplish the same thing, they may feel inspired to persevere in their own weaknesses.
- I am not such an intelligent student for a guy in a wheelchair who earned both his bachelor's and master's degrees. Book smarts never came naturally to me. Rather, I relied on Jesus while spending a lot of time in the library.
- I am not a gifted evangelist with a knack for meeting people and being able to hold their rapt attention with what I say about Jesus. Rather, my slow and slurred speech inadvertently beckons listeners to stop. Then they begin investing their time into listening to me. When someone invests their most precious resource, they tend to hang out to see its results. Then they're eventually told the good news of Jesus Christ.

Looking back to when I first sent out cover letters of my own, I knew I couldn't open with: "My name is Todd Lollar. I'm a slow-moving, slower-talking, speech-impeded, prolonged-achieving, mobilized-in-a-wheelchair, cerebral-palsied minister of the gospel. But people listen to me."

Then again, maybe I should have.

It would have saved me from a lot of pain and tears.

Experiencing Discrimination

Being rejected for job after job wouldn't have been so difficult were it not for the fact that I consistently made it into their final candidate pool. I believe I arrived there because I had well-known references, ample field experience, and the skills required for these particular positions.

But then the phone interviews would happen.

"Hello, is this Mr. Lollar."

"Y . . . y . . . yes."

A slight pause would sometimes occur, followed by, "Mr. Lollar, are you there?"

"Y . . . y . . . yes."

"This is Mr. Hiring Guy with That Ministry You Applied To. I'm excited to talk to you. We've reviewed your resume and cover letter, and we really like what we've read. I'd just like to ask you a few follow-up questions."

"O . . . K."

"Great. Now, can you share some specific times about evangelizing some of the students at LSU?"

"I'd be . . . glad to. I remember . . . this one time . . . a . . . a . . . about a year ago . . . when . . ."

If I weren't interrupted halfway through my first sentence, I'd often hear a long pause after finishing my sentence. In time, I learned that the long, silent reply indicated that I'd been thrown out of the interview process. None of the hiring personnel could hear past my belabored words to understand my heart and my desire to see lives changed through the gospel. Maybe if they could have met me in person, it would have been different.

After I told one interviewer about my CP, he even said, "Wow, Todd! I didn't know. I don't think that, with your disease, you could do this job."

I'm not sure what I said in reply, but I thought, "*What?! I have a disease? I better set up an appointment with my doc ASAP!*" (Of course, CP is not a disease.)

With so much rejection, I felt that all my hard work in school and during my internship was for nothing. These hiring personnel saw me as qualified for their positions based on my resume and references. They would even rave about my giftedness and accomplishments in certain areas.

Had they given me the chance, I would have told them that my time spent as an interim minister at LSU was amazing. When I told LSU I believed God was calling me elsewhere, they'd wanted me to stay. They'd seen that year as a great year for the campus ministry organization.

So, people wanted me—just not the people on the phone. They couldn't get past my obvious weaknesses, which was ironic, because I knew that my weaknesses were the only reasons I'd been able to accomplish anything in ministry.

Didn't these Christian leaders understand the power of weakness?

The Single Reason I Believe I Was Passed Over for So Many Jobs

Of course, the ultimate example of the strength of weakness is Jesus. God boldly proclaimed that truth through his Son by letting

Jesus become weak on the cross. Yet through God's power, Jesus rose from the grave three days later. There's no better illustration of the upside-down way God works in this world, which is so focused on power and strength as defining characteristics.

For years, I was mad—maybe angry is a better word—at those people who had vaulted me to the tops of their lists only to strike me off once they heard my voice or learned of my disability. But I was healed of those wounds at the foot of the cross. When God shed his forgiveness through his weakness on the cross over me, I began to see these "afflicters" in a different light. I recalled that Christ showed compassion to those who patronized him and exploited him, even acknowledging their ignorance of his ultimate power by saying, "Father, forgive them; for they do not know what they are doing" (Luke 23:34).

I realized that many of these leaders might have been discriminating against me because *they* didn't have room in their own lives, careers, and leadership to be vulnerable and transparent about *their* weaknesses. Because their perspectives on their own weaknesses had yet to be redefined, their views on other people's weaknesses were limited—or even nonexistent. I believe this fact is the number one detriment to any company and organization, Christian or not. Without the freedom to be weak, leaders lead from atop a house of cards that's bound to fall.

Even in the Christian realm, leadership development is focused on capitalizing one's strengths and minimizing one's weaknesses. We're subtly coerced into creating resumes and cover letters that copy what the culture around us cares about instead of crafting vulnerable letters like Dusty's, which boast about the unvarnished truth of our weaknesses as human beings. To be proud of our strengths is so opposite of how God's kingdom works. God's kingdom is upside down from the world's perspective. Weakness is the catalyst through which God's power moves in your career, family, ministry, and relationships. Since everything changed at Calvary, weak is the new strong!

Can you imagine what a culture that celebrates both strengths *and* weaknesses would look like? If our Christian organizations and nonprofits could truly achieve that state, I believe we'd see more thriving churches, Christian organizations, ministries, and even companies that expand God's kingdom because they would no longer be relying on their own human strength—which means their own human limitations—but, because they would understand their individual and corporate weaknesses, they would be relying on God's power.

I pray that today's Christian organizations would be different from today's corporate culture. I pray that they could allow their leaders to be radically transparent about their shortcomings. I think the church-at-large sometimes forgets that pastors are still humans too. They shouldn't be burdened with the expectation of perfection. No person should have to shoulder such a heavy burden. But our Christian organizations and the church—the body of Christ—need to be the leaders in removing that burden from our leadership.

People become what their leaders model. If leaders don't model transparency in weakness, neither will their followers. Consequently, the organization will miss out on the propelling momentum found in leading from vulnerability.

We need to allow our leaders to admit their weaknesses so that God, through his church, might then strengthen his servants and people. When God's power touches people with his love and his leaders are allowed to express their giftedness freely, God's people will certainly be blessed with depth and growth because the leaders will then be functioning as conduits of God's power.

I Was Guilty of Discrimination Too

Some hiring personnel discriminated against me during my early professional ministry days. But I was also discriminating against them and looking down on them for their lack of understanding what I thought was such an evident truth in the Bible: that God loves using the weak. God helped me overcome my anger toward them by showing me that I was still like them—that I was narrow-minded in how I regarded their worldview.

According to the Oxford dictionary, discrimination is "the unjust or prejudicial treatment of different categories of people or things, especially on the grounds of race, age, or sex." But discrimination is not limited to those categories. Humans are capable of discrimination toward others based on a broad set of characteristics. Unjust intolerance can evolve from anyone's narrow-mindedness on just about any topic.

And we've all dealt with discrimination in some form or another, whether as the one doing the discriminating or the one being discriminated against. I must admit that I used to prejudge a person when I knew they didn't have as much education as I have. Today, I see others without a certain level of institutional education as a major asset to the organization I lead because they often have more creative solutions to problems and understand how those who are likewise outside of a college institution think. In other words, I better understand that "God has placed the members, each one of them, in the body, just as He desired" (1 Cor. 12:18). God created each of us with specific skills, strengths, *and weaknesses* to be used by him.

Yet I believe the church is still quick to look at people the way the world looks at people. With how visual our society is, it's hard not to. The world celebrates good looks, photoshopped women, and muscle-bound men. The world considers a person's exterior long before inquiring about their interior. I fear that God's people—and by that I mean you and me—do the same. But this is so contrary to the gospel. We must stop looking through the lens of strength and instead discover the potential in overlooked people who boast in their weaknesses.

This is how God operates. He did so throughout the Bible, and he continues to do so today. In fact, Paul implores us to do the same: "Therefore from now on we recognize no one according to the flesh; even though we have known Christ according to the flesh, yet now we know Him in this way no longer. Therefore if anyone is in Christ, he is a new creature; the old things passed away; behold, new things have come" (2 Cor. 5:16–17). Here's the Todd Lollar version: we see no one according to their weakness but according to God's power that is at work in them.

What's the key to seeing past someone's weaknesses? To view people *in Christ*. To see them through his eyes as *a new creation*.

> We ought to view weaknesses as a way that we will excel in our heavenly vocations in God's kingdom.

We ought to view others as though they're Adam or Eve in the Garden of Eden before weakness entered the world because of the fall. We ought to view everyone with purpose through these "new creation" eyes. We ought to see others as new creations with God-given roles, gifts, and attributes, just like those God gave to Adam and Eve.

God holds us to a higher standard, calling us to see others and their weaknesses with the renewed eyes of Christ in us. We should work to recognize others the way God sees them so that his power can be seen through their weakness. We should celebrate their weaknesses as strengths, just as we hope others will see our weaknesses as strengths too. I'm not bound by a wheelchair; I'm *mobilized* in a wheelchair. We should not only celebrate weaknesses but also *mobilize* others in their weaknesses, knowing they are a vehicle for God's power!

We ought to view weaknesses as a way that we will excel in our heavenly vocations in God's kingdom. When we view people from the perspective of their heavenly roles, we won't regard their earthly imperfections. Rather, we'll see them as Jesus sees us: a new creation restored to life and purpose as his image-bearers on earth.

To see others as Jesus sees us ought always to be our goal. This is how discrimination and prejudice dissipate in our world today.

But that first demands knowing how Jesus sees you.

Incredibly, he sees your weakness, but he also sees your usefulness, your value, and your worthiness to contribute to his kingdom, no matter your strengths *or* your weaknesses. When you begin to see yourself as Christ sees you, you can then begin to partake in the cultivation of his kingdom on earth as it is in heaven.

The Odd Truth about Compassionate Living

If you've been freed to live free indeed (John 8:36), you must come to understand that others may still be shackled by their weaknesses—even other Christians. What do I mean by this?

I view my CP as a strength. People who know me well can testify to that fact. But that doesn't mean that everyone with whom I interact knows this. Instead, they naively see my CP as a severe limitation. They prejudge me based on what they can see, hear, and experience when in my presence. So what they observe about me is always filtered through their prior knowledge of "people like me."

For instance, some people try to connect with me by saying things like, "I have a cousin with multiple sclerosis." Immediately, I'll think my reply: *MS is horribly degenerative. It's nothing like CP! Get your disabilities straight. In fact, the way I stay active is through the power of God, and my disability, posture, and speech fluency have all improved over time.* I know the person means well, but it's still frustrating to hear things like that.

If other people don't assume the worst about me, they sometimes feel the need to patronize me, as if I were a child who can't take care of himself. This comes out in questions like, "Do you live with your family?" In their mind, I assume, "family" is a mom and dad who take care of me. They assume I can't take care of myself, so I think they're a little shocked when I answer, "Yes, my wife, son, daughter, and I all live together in the house that I work to pay the mortgage on." Well, I'm probably not that blunt, but I sometimes think such an answer. I'll also hear things like, "Wow, you do well for yourself," or, "I'm glad to see you out and about," when I'm doing what most people would consider normal, everyday routines, like going to a coffee shop.

> If they can't see their own weaknesses as something to boast in for the glory of God, then they certainly won't be able to see that in others.

Again, these patronizing words stem from well-meaning people who just don't know me. But it still hurts because it underscores *their* belief that my weakness is truly a weakness. This gets to the heart of being set free to be free indeed. Even though *I* may have been set free to see my greatest weakness as my greatest strength, other people may not have arrived at that destination in their own lives. And if they can't see their own weaknesses as something to boast in for the glory of God, then they certainly won't be able to see that in others.

But I hope this book will help with that.

This isn't a new experience, either. Do you know how the Jews treated the apostles Peter and John when they began preaching about Jesus following his ascension? "Now as they observed the confidence of Peter and John and understood that they were *uneducated and untrained men*, they were amazed, and began to recognize them as having been with Jesus" (Acts 4:13—emphasis mine). The Jews were amazed because they couldn't reconcile their judgments of the "uneducated and untrained men" with the confident men who were proclaiming the gospel in front of them. Yet again, God took a weakness and transformed it into a strength.

Their amazement prods them to ask why these men are now the way they are. People wonder the same thing about me and my ministry: "How can you, with CP or MS or whatever, do what you do with such joy?" When I hear a question like that, I always recall, "Always be ready to tell everyone who asks you why you believe as you do. Be gentle as you speak and show respect" (1 Pet. 3:15b NLV). I see their question as an opportunity to share the good news of Jesus, that he died *in weakness* that we might have victory.

But it took me a long time to mature into taking advantage of those kinds of opportunities and to be gentle and respectful. God had to grow me into a believer who wouldn't get hung up or offended when someone else didn't see me the way I see myself. Rather, God helped me see that he could use those moments of misunderstanding my weakness to help others see how he could likewise transform *their* weaknesses into their strengths.

Again, a lesson Dusty taught me long ago comes to mind: just because God reveals something to you does not mean others have been open to seeing, hearing, and acting upon the same. Sometimes, God's revelation is meant for you alone, and it takes others longer to view their weaknesses as their strengths.

Following Christ Means Realizing Your Weakness

Christ willingly chose death because he was responding to God rather than man. He knew the full extent of *all* of our weaknesses and still chose to redeem us. If that's not a magnificent truth, I don't know what is. It's this kind of upside-down love that compels me to live out the redefined life God has given me rather than react to other people's misperceptions about my weaknesses.

When I begin to get upset about how others may view my weakness, I remember, "Consider him who endured such hostility from sinners, so that you will not grow weary and lose heart" (Heb. 12:3 NIV). Jesus's humility inspires me to react with compassion, not anger or frustration. As they preached the gospel, the apostles modeled this behavior as well: "But Peter and the apostles answered, 'We must obey God rather than men'" (Acts 5:29). In the face of other people's misperceptions of our weaknesses, respond in view of what God thinks and not how humans perceive your weaknesses.

If you're discriminated against because of your weakness and you experience closed doors despite God's gifting to lead you through those doors, obey God rather than men. By God's power, continue to pursue your calling.

If you are patronized for your weakness, obey God rather than men. See their shortsightedness as an opportunity to speak truth into that person's life so that they might be freed from their poor theology about weakness in a Christian's life.

If others thrust their opinions and experiences on you about how they think you ought to cope with your weaknesses, choose to live by God's transformative definition of your weaknesses. To react defensively or angrily is to fall into bad habits from your former life. Remember: you are a new creation.

The answer to being freed from others' small and earthbound view of weakness is to see Jesus defeating Satan and the sin of the world through his willful weakness on the cross, a place where he gave victory to all of his weak children that we might see ourselves as weak within but strong with him. That's the kind of faith Dusty had, and I'm so glad God placed me in his life at just that time so

I could learn that lesson too. His example set me up for daily life in transparency of my redefined weakness.

After much rejection, I tenaciously pursued an open door with a Christian organization. They knew of my prior ministry work. They knew of my CP and my speech disfluency. They knew of my perceived limitations, but they saw beyond my weaknesses. They read the resume of my life, and rather than seeing what every other hiring organization had seen (or heard), they opened a door so I could roll through it. They saw my weaknesses as a conduit for God's power to travel through me and into the lives of the men and women they wanted to reach.

Transparency with your weakness wins hearts, because everyone is weak. God makes it worth it to hang in there. Who knows? God just might use you to free the person who focused on your weakness from their own insecurities. Your transparency might just be what they need to experience God's power through their weaknesses too!

Thank you, God—and thank you, too, Dusty.

CHAPTER 5

A WEAK PRAYER TO MEET BONO

"The Spirit also helps our weakness; for we do not know how to pray as we should, but the Spirit Himself intercedes for us with groanings too deep for words."

—Romans 8:26

"I pray to get to know the will of God, because then the prayers have more chance of coming true."[1]

Those aren't words spoken by a well-known pastor. They weren't written by a best-selling inspirational author. But they were spoken by someone who is an inspiring, well-known best seller.

In a 2013 interview for the Irish TV series "The Meaning of Life," interviewer Gay Bryne asked his guest, "Do you pray . . . and what do you pray for?"

That's when U2 front man Bono delivered his answer: "I pray to get to know the will of God."

And that's only one of a dozen reasons I love U2.

Hearing from God through Alternative Rock

It took me over a decade to discover my first love in music: U2. But when I did, I went on a devouring spree of everything they made. I first became a fan with the 1991 release of their seventh studio album, *Achtung Baby*, which was a noticeable departure in sound and style from the massive best-selling albums that preceded it, *The Joshua Tree* and *Rattle and Hum*. *Achtung Baby* features some of their greatest songs, or, at least, my personal favorites, like "Until the End of the World," "Ultra Violet (Light My Way)," and "The Fly."

My U2 admiration runs deep because God has used their music to touch my heart and consistently deepen my relationship with Jesus. The more I listen to their lyrics, the more I hear how almost every one of their songs is about Jesus and faith. Just as The Edge's indelible guitar work makes you instantly know it's a U2 song, so too does the proliferation of Scripture throughout their lyrics. Sometimes it's subtle, but not often. Just listen to "40" from their third album, *War*, or read through the impressive list of fifty-plus Bible references in their songs on the fan site @u2.[2]

Like millions of other fans, their songs compelled me because the lyrics weren't overtly religious. Rather than being preached to, I felt ministered to. Their music seemed to always speak to me right where I was in my relationship with Jesus.

And when I finally got the opportunity to experience a U2 concert in person, I realized I'd shown up at a worship service! In fact—am I allowed to say this?—the most worshipful moments I've ever experienced have happened at U2 shows. (And no, I wasn't worshiping Bono!) They worshiped God in a way that spoke to me and at a level at which I could connect to them and to God through their considerable talents.

U2's ability to fill stadiums and touch millions of lost hearts with the gospel amazed me. Their covert-yet-overt evangelism appealed to my calling to see God work in others' lives. I couldn't understand how they could hold such huge secular audiences in rapt attention for hours on end while essentially leading a worship service. Only God's work could do something like that.

And, considering my cerebral palsy and everything else you already know about me by now, I was overjoyed that they openly sang about their weaknesses. Even though these men were in one of the most successful bands of all time, they still knew they were just four blokes from Dublin.

Bono, short for "Bono Vox," or "good voice," is a loud public voice when it comes to his need for Christ. Bonavox was the name of a hearing aid store on a street near where a young Bono attended youth group.[3] What irony that such a gifted voice received his name from a place that helped the deaf to hear; from weakness comes strength. As a guy with a speech impediment, I'm encouraged by this piece of U2 trivia. How Bono got his name displays God's power through weakness!

If only I could meet him. What a wild, far-fetched dream!

I'd let him know that through their weaknesses, I'd found strength in my faith.

And what I needed strength in may surprise you.

I'm a terrible prayer.

A Weak Prayer

I know I'm not alone when it comes to being a weak prayer. What do I mean by that?

A weak prayer is someone who's inconsistent. Maybe they mean well and even set aside time on their daily calendar for five minutes of prayer, but that time always seems to get replaced by something more pressing.

A weak prayer is someone who prays without intent. They offer vague prayers for family members, friends, and coworkers—"Bless them. Be with them. Heal them."—and mark "prayer" off their mental to-do list. They fail to pray with the intent of truly connecting with God. And they often fail to pray with the intent of baring themselves before God. A weak prayer prays for others because that's often easier than praying for himself.

A weak prayer is someone who doesn't really believe God will answer her prayers. They try to have faith, but past life experiences and unmet expectations temper their prayers with an unhealthy dose of material reality. A weak prayer is one who has trouble praying in faith even after Jesus, God himself, has proclaimed endless possibility.

For example, take the conversation between Jesus and a father right before Jesus delivers the man's son from an unclean spirit by healing his deafness and muteness: "And Jesus said to him, "'If You can?' All things are possible to him who believes.' Immediately the boy's father cried out and said, 'I do believe; help my unbelief'" (Mark 9:23–24).

A weak prayer is also someone who fails to act upon her prayers. She forgets that prayer is a two-way street where God wants her to do her part so he can do his part. She forgets, "Even so faith, if it has no works, is dead, being by itself" (James 2:17). A weak prayer asks God to accomplish something huge in her life but fails to step out in faith to see that huge thing happen. A weak prayer forgets that our faith actually ignites God's power. I love instances when Jesus heals a weak person, like a blind man, and Jesus responds, "Your faith has made you well" (Luke 17:19).

I'm guilty of all of those spiritual lapses. But God met me in my weakness and taught me an unforgettable lesson on prayer that sparked my passion for the power of prayer in my life.

And I'll bet you'll never guess whom he used to do so.

To Live beyond Myself

To me, Bono may be the greatest evangelist of our day. He probably wouldn't compare himself to the apostle Paul or Billy Graham, but he's no doubt an evangelist with a worldwide reach who's not afraid to preach the truth.

I was particularly convinced of that fact following the 2004 release of *How to Dismantle an Atomic Bomb*, an album I nicknamed "the social justice worship album." Through the lyrics in those songs, Bono invited his listeners to become more aware of the weak and wounded. He begged for the rich to help the poor and the healthy to aid the sick. He called the world to take notice and take responsibility for the plight of AIDS that was ravaging Africa (and still is). He sang for unity in helping the helpless. He called the world to love one another, just as Christ said two thousand years earlier: "This is My commandment, that you love one another, just as I have loved you" (John 15:12).

As a result of writing that album, Bono cofounded ONE, "a campaigning and advocacy organisation of nearly eight million people around the world taking action to end extreme poverty and preventable disease, particularly in Africa."[4] Millions joined this campaign of making the weak strong. Celebrities lent their voices and platforms to encourage others to take action, both from their homes in the United States and to travel abroad to help those less fortunate than themselves. To scan ONE's ten-year retrospective website is to see impressive numbers and witness the even more impressive work that a God-led spark in Bono's spiritual life made real.[5]

The way Bono invited others to live beyond themselves reminded me of Jesus's call to the fishermen, tradesmen, and one tax collector who would become his disciples. Through their brief but incredible time with Jesus during his three-year ministry on earth, the disciples conducted their own follow-the-One campaign and saw the sick healed, the oppressed freed, the hungry fed, and the dead risen. Denying self, they experienced a life beyond themselves, their weaknesses wrapped in the power of God. That kind of life is within our grasp as well, but we often need someone to call it out of us. U2's convicting, Jesus-centered, and compassion-filled lyrics moved me to live a life beyond myself and my weaknesses and to love Jesus and others with all I am.

That's why I see Bono as such a great evangelist. It's not just that he's vocal about his faith to millions, but he practices what he preaches. If I had to guess, he's not a weak prayer at all. He seems to always be on the move on that two-way street of prayer and always stepping out in faith to see what God wants to do with him next.

When I saw and heard about all that Bono was doing for the world in 2004, I quietly thought to myself, *I'd like to meet him someday, just to say thanks for what he's given me through his lyrics and given the world through his obedience to God.*

But I also thought, *That's ridiculous, Todd. He's* Bono. *You're just Todd.*

Then another voice spoke up: *Why don't you pray about it?*

I replied with a laugh. *Pray about* that? *Can I pray for something like that?*

Well, the first step is to pray. You remember how to do that?

Bothering God

Considering that my life began with my mother's prayer to keep me alive shortly after my birth, some may find it surprising that I struggled to pray well for most of my life. Others may see my cerebral palsy, speech impediment, and the other challenges have and think I must pray all the time.

I hate to be the one to tell you, but that was rarely the case. I can confidently say that I'm a more consistent prayer now, but I'm also still human and still wrestle with making time for prayer.

Sometimes, it's not so much about the time. Rather, it's about my arrogant belief that I can handle most of my life on my own. I try to figure out my troubles, challenges, and concerns through problem-solving techniques that ultimately fail. I consider all my options, graph out the pros and cons, and then look at my problem through the lens of the most insidious of worldly philosophies: What's the best decision *for me*?

In other words, I try to take care of the problem so Jesus doesn't have to. Why should I bother God with something so inconsequential as how I'm going to get on that airplane in a week, or where my next paycheck will come from, or how I should reply to a coworker after a serious disagreement?

Of course, none of those issues is inconsequential. You may even consider some of them to be highly consequential, and, therefore, they should matter more to God. But we so often forget that it's *all* important to God because *you* are all-important to God. Think of it this way: Christ didn't die *only* for your biggest issues. He died for *you*. And *you* encompass everything you are, from the smallest worry to the deepest fear. God listens to our prayers and cares about each one of them. God is for you: "What then shall we say to these things? If God is for us, who is against us?" (Rom. 8:31).

When we pray from weak theology and weaker belief, we miss out on relying on the One who is all-powerful. We fail to realize the incredible truth that God "is able to do far more abundantly beyond all that we ask or think, according to the power that works within us" through our weaknesses (Eph. 3:20).

Read that verse again.

Do you really believe what it says? If he's truly able to do "far more abundantly beyond all that we ask or think," what have you been asking or thinking lately? No prayer is too small, or too big, for God. But what about praying to meet Bono?

Annoying God

I'll never forget when I saw U2 in 2005 during their *Vertigo* tour. It was the greatest worship event I've ever attended. My already sky-high admiration for the band and for Bono somehow reached into the stratosphere after that experience.

Following that show, I asked God, "Would you give me an opportunity to meet Bono so I can tell him in person what he's meant to my faith? Would you open a door for me to meet him?"

Even as I prayed, I felt doubt. My spiritual weakness in prayer kept whispering that my chances of meeting Bono were as low as my chances of meeting the president. Still, I continued to pray in the days, months, and years after that for the same once-in-a-lifetime opportunity. Whenever my doubts would creep back into my thoughts, God would remind me of the many amazing things he'd already accomplished in my life. In those moments, I'd realize that God, if he wanted to, had the power to bring Bono to my very doorstep. If he could do the miraculous, like part the Red Sea and allow my little baby-self to keep breathing, then he could do the ridiculous, like allowing me to meet one of my spiritual heroes.

I learned an important lesson about prayer when I began asking the Good Shepherd if I could meet the Good Voice: persistence. Unlike most people I know, it seems that God *likes* being bugged. If you doubt that, consider what Jesus said: "Keep on asking, and you will receive what you ask for. Keep on seeking, and you will find. Keep on knocking, and the door will be opened to you. For everyone who asks, receives. Everyone who seeks, finds. And to everyone who knocks, the door will be opened" (Matt. 7:7–8 NLT).

Maybe God's ultimate goal wasn't to let me meet Bono. Maybe it was to teach me (and now you) about prayer—to strengthen me in what may have been my greatest spiritual weakness. Maybe I was never going to meet the man who'd influenced my Christian life in such a deep way. Maybe I would have to say goodbye to that dream.

But then I went to another U2 concert in October of 2009. After four years of fairly consistent prayer, I was sure I was about to meet Bono Vox.

The Moment Arrives

The AT&T Stadium in Arlington, Texas, the home of the Dallas Cowboys, is gigantic. It's currently the fourth-largest stadium in the NFL and can hold eighty thousand fans. I don't know how many people were at the U2 show for their 360° Tour, but it sure felt like the place was packed, including the field.

A few weeks before the event, I received a call that the organizers had reconfigured the stage, so I needed to pick up new tickets. I didn't know until the night of the show where I'd be sitting. As an attendant guided my friend and me to our seats, we kept getting closer and closer to the stage. My eyes got wider and wider.

We stopped at the forty-yard line.

Front row.

As close as we could possibly get.

I felt as if they were daring us to walk onto the stage.

I thought, *Thank you, God!*

During the incredible concert, I kept feeling the prompting of the Holy Spirit to do something to make my long-held prayer a reality. As I've said before, God was teaching me more and more about prayer, and one of those lessons was about the faith I needed to exert so that God might be able to answer my prayers. In other words, I needed to move so he could move. I'd already asked and sought; now I needed to knock.

Consequently, I kept rolling back to the nearby VIP area to see if I could sneak backstage and meet Bono. I talked to as many official-looking people as I could. I eavesdropped on conversations to see who might have authority to get me into the cordoned-off areas. Eventually, I heard a woman who worked in the VIP section say something about Bono's assistant. My ears perked up. I felt the Holy Spirit prompt me to talk to her. My wheels immediately spun in her direction.

Maybe this was going to be The Moment.

"Hi . . . I'm Todd . . . Bono has meant . . . so much . . . to my walk . . . with God. Do you think . . . I could . . . meet him?" In that dark corridor, I was hoping she could light my way toward this long-held dream.

Gratefully, she patiently listened to me. "Let me see if that can be arranged. Just wait here."

Those were the longest couple of minutes in my life.

When she returned, she kindly said, "I'm sorry, Todd. Bono's assistant said it's just not possible."

I wasn't devastated, but I was disappointed. I was so sure this was my opportunity. I really thought God was going to answer my prayer because I'd been so persistent in praying and rolling by faith, putting faith to action and acting on the prompting of the Holy Spirit to make myself available for God to move.

But God didn't move in that moment, or at least he didn't move in the way I wanted him to, which was probably another lesson I needed to be taught about prayer.

I rolled back to Jeremy and shook my head in a moment of surrender. "They don't . . . have time for me. But . . . how can I be sad . . . about that? We just saw U2 . . . up close and personal!"

I was thrilled to have attended that concert; but on the ride home, I tried to overcome my disappointment. I'd been so close and doubted I'd ever be that close again. With a small laugh, I realized, *I still haven't found what I'm looking for.*

Still, I prayed that God would make such a meeting happen someday between now and until the end of the world.

Still, I kept seeking and knocking.

Still, I kept learning about prayer.

Frustrated Prayers

Honestly, at that point, I felt defeated. I knew that asking to meet Bono was a somewhat selfish prayer and that there were so many other things I could be praying for—and I did—but what are you supposed to do when your heartfelt prayers seem to go unanswered? What can you do when you feel as if praying is, well, frustrating?

First, know that when you pray, sometimes you don't need to know what you're praying for. I know that doesn't make sense, but consider what the apostle Paul wrote in Romans 8:

> And the Holy Spirit helps us *in our weakness*. For example, we don't know what God wants us to pray for. But the Holy Spirit prays for us with groanings that cannot be expressed in words. And the Father who knows all hearts knows what the Spirit is saying, for the Spirit pleads for us believers in harmony with God's own will. . . . Who dares accuse us whom God has chosen for his own? No one—for God himself has given us right standing with himself. Who then will condemn us? No one—for Christ Jesus died for us and was raised to life for us, and he is sitting in the place of honor at God's

right hand, pleading for us. (Rom. 8:26–27, 33–34 NLT—
emphasis mine)

Do you struggle to get the "right" words out when you pray? Do
you feel incapable of putting your thoughts and feelings into words?
Do you feel self-conscious when you pray out loud? When you're
overcome with emotion, can you even find any words to say?

Welcome to my world! Your prayer life is like my speech
impediment.

So what's the answer? Having a relationship with someone who
knows your every weakness. For instance, my wife understands
me. Now, she may not always understand *why* I'm saying what
I'm saying, but she understands what I'm saying. Why? Because
we've spent a lot of time together and she loves me. She wants to
understand me so that she can know me better, and vice versa.

It's the same way with prayer. God knows our struggles as
weak, imperfect, and sometimes less-than-faithful believers. But
he understands our hearts and minds better than we do, because
he created us and he loves us. We trust that we "pray the will of
God," because God has transformed our minds and has given us
the mind of Christ. By spending time with him, we gain confidence in him, and we start to be emboldened by faith that God is
working through our weak prayers. When you reach out to God,
he's immediately ready to reach back, like a loving father who
desperately misses his long-lost child. In fact, God so longs to
speak into our lives that he's given us two not-so-secret agents to
help us pray.

First, the Holy Spirit strengthens us in our weakness of prayer.
If all your prayers turn into whining, complaining, moaning, and
groaning—that's okay! The Spirit pleads to God on your behalf.
He knows exactly how to interpret your prayers into something
God understands. Whether or not you think you're praying "right,"

you always have a translator with God. Personally, this affirms me. I know that sometimes I need a translator on earth because of my stuttering and slurring—even with people who speak English! (That fact makes me LMWO—laugh my wheels off.)

The Spirit knows the will of God. He prays for you. Like the best advocate you could find, he speaks on your behalf. And he knows how to interpret weak words to the One who has the power to respond to you with unstoppable action. The Holy Spirit, as part of the Trinity, lives in harmony with the will of God. Realize this truth and relax your need to pray "right." The Spirit will help you in your weaknesses; and the more you pray, the more help you'll receive, and your prayer life will become more energized.

The second not-so-secret agent helping a weak prayer is Jesus. Because of his sacrifice, we now have direct access to God. We can't forget how earth shattering that fact is. In fact, the Bible even records that parts of the earth literally shattered when Jesus died on the cross: "Then Jesus shouted out again, and he released his spirit. At that moment the curtain in the sanctuary of the Temple was torn in two, from top to bottom" (Matt. 27:50–51 NLT). In Jesus's weakness of releasing his spirit, he opened the communication line between you and God.

To my fellow weak prayers: Believe that the Holy Spirit intercedes for you, even when you are weak and have no idea what to say. Believe that Jesus is your direct access to God. Believe that they both want you to know what God's will is for your life. Believe, and pray—and don't forget to act, either.

Oh yes: a weak prayer acts on what they pray!

The Moment Arrives, Part 2

Only a week had passed since I'd nearly met Bono. Determined to see if I'd ever get to meet the man, I went to another U2 show in Norman, Oklahoma.

By this point, especially since I'd come so close at the last concert, my family and friends knew that I'd been praying to meet Bono. They joined with me in that prayer. I understood that sharing a spiritual weakness with others, such as my lackluster prayer life, could allow others to strengthen me in that particular weakness. I was encouraged by their prayers on my behalf, and it made me pray all the more for this opportunity.

During that time, I realized another truth about prayer: the more we pray, the more God wants us to become an active part in what only God can make possible. A weak prayer may result in a strong answer when we move by faith to seek and knock. Like Bono said, that's when "the prayers have more chance of coming true."

> A weak prayer may result in a strong answer when we move by faith to seek and knock.

If I ever wanted to meet Bono, I'd have to do something about it. I couldn't just wait for Bono to show up at my front door. So I trekked to Norman with my friend Tracy. Our seats were in the wheelchair section of the End Zone at the Gaylord Family Oklahoma Memorial Stadium. Because I'd attended so many OU football games as a student, I knew this stadium like I knew every word to the U2 *Achtung Baby* album. Back then, I'd hang out in the field house while visiting with my friends on the football team. And the field house—where U2 was surely preparing—was right under our seats.

Before the show, I looked to my left for the ramp leading to the field house. It was blocked by concertgoers and backstage security. Soon, the show began, and the opening band went onstage.

I glanced to my left again. The crowd had thinned. I could see the ramp.

I felt the Holy Spirit, the one who interceded for me in my weak prayers, quickly and directly speak to my heart: *Go now!*

I rolled out of my section without telling anyone what I was doing.

I tried to keep my hopes, and my heartbeat, down.

I wheeled past the attendants and to the front door of the field house. A dozen or so tour employees stood in my way, but no one asked me to leave. I'm not even sure they noticed me, which was surprising. As the guy in the wheelchair, I'm used to being noticed.

Not knowing what to do, I did what I'd done since I'd begun praying to meet Bono: I waited. The Holy Spirit's prompting was stronger than what I'd felt in Dallas. I knew this had to be the moment. I just needed to be patient. Again.

A guy with dreadlocks finally asked me what I was waiting for.

"I'm hoping to . . . go backstage . . . and meet Bono."

He chuckled. "There's no way, man. Sorry."

I told him how much the band had affected my life, but he didn't relent.

Disappointed and not wanting to miss when the band went onstage, I rolled back toward my seat. I was feeling frustrated because the Holy Spirit's prompting had felt so strong. *How could this not be the moment?*

I consoled myself with the thought that maybe I'd have a chance after the show.

As I wheeled myself back to my seat, I momentarily glanced to my right just before I reached the gate exiting backstage, and caught the unmistakable profile of an image I will never forget: less than a foot from me, the front man for U2, conceivably the world's greatest band led by the world's greatest evangelist, stood beside me in a boxer's hoodie and no sunglasses. He bent forward so we were eye to eye.

This was the moment.

I stopped. I put out my right hand. I said, "Hi, Bono. I'm Todd Lollar."

With a warm smile and a firm grip, he shook my hand.

Miraculously, without a slur or a stutter, I said, "Bono, God has used you in my life and ministry in amazing ways."

Bono bent forward, said, "God bless you," and hugged me.

Dazed from this incredible experience, it took me more than a few moments to realize The Edge, U2's inimitable lead guitarist, was standing right next to Bono. The Edge bent forward and shook my hand too. Not only had God answered my prayer—I met Bono—he did "far more abundantly beyond all that we ask or think" and allowed me to meet The Edge, too.

That experience was more than just meeting a couple of rock stars. It felt like I'd met two older brothers in Christ who impacted my faith in profound ways.

I finally rolled back to my seat. I couldn't help but yell, "I met Bono! I met Bono!" for at least a couple of minutes. My only regret is that I forgot to take a picture despite my cell phone having been on my lap during the entire experience. Blame it the surreal excitement of the situation, as if I'd taken some kind of miracle drug. But, honestly, the picture in my mind, which will never fade as long as I live, is more important to me. That mental photo of meeting Bono and The Edge is more than just a cool moment in my life— it's a lasting testament to God's faithfulness when we pray, even in weakness. It's a reminder of how God used a strange prayer request to draw me closer to him and to teach me truths about relating to him in prayer.

Today, I don't pray to meet Bono.

I pray to know the will of God.

Notes

[1] Antonia Blumberg, "U2's Bono Opens Up about Jesus, God and Praying with His Kids," *Huffpost*, April 11, 2014, http://www.huffingtonpost.com/2014 /04/11/bono-jesus_n_5127614.html.

[2] "Bible References in U2 Lyrics from @U2," https://www.atu2.com/lyrics /biblerefs.html.

[3] "U2 Travelguide: Bonavox," http://www.u2tour.de/travelguide/guides/en /Bonavox_Hearing_Aid_Store.html.

[4] "About ONE," ONE, https://www.one.org/international/about/.

[5] "About ONE," ONE, https://www.one.org/10years/.

CHAPTER 6

WEAKNESS DESTROYS BARRIERS

"A renewal in which there is no distinction between Greek and Jew, circumcised and uncircumcised, barbarian, Scythian, slave and freeman, but Christ is all, and in all."

—Colossians 3:11

I can drive, but my driving isn't the best. Even in graduate school, I was seldom surprised when another driver would give me a one-finger salute. I'll let you guess which finger they used.

One of these instances was more memorable than the rest. I was on my way to a pizza place for lunch when I inadvertently cut someone off. The guys in that truck, who looked like they might have also been students, swerved around me and let all their middle fingers fly.

They caught me on a day when I'd had a great quiet time with Jesus. I was seeing people how he sees people. I just prayed, "Lord, use those fingers for your glory."

Not too much later, I pulled into the parking lot at the pizza place and rolled into the restaurant. My eyes immediately gravitated toward the loud group of four guys in the corner, all wearing Sub T-16 T-shirts.

Their middle fingers were no longer covering their faces so I could tell: they were students too. And because ACU isn't that big of a university, I knew they knew me.

Weakness Breaks Down the Walls of Stereotypes

To properly set the scene, some background information is necessary. The Sub T-16 fraternity was established at Abilene Christian University in 1923. Its motto is "To stimulate a closer bond of friendship, loyalty to the school, stimulate social activities and bring about a greater appreciation of the real values of life."

Of course, "the real values of life" is open to interpretation. Ostensibly, ACU is a Christian school. *Christian* is even the school's middle name! But this fraternal organization of young men, at least during my years of being an ACU Wildcat, were anything but Christian. Their "real values of life" seemed more like the real values of *Animal House*.

As far as I'd heard, they smoked, dipped, drank, and hooked up. They were your stereotypical college fraternity of boys acting like men who wanted to remain boys who shaved. To further ostracize themselves, whether purposefully or not, they adored the Confederate flag and proudly displayed rebel flags in their homes and apartments. They loved Texas and the south, which most Texans do, but I'd say they loved it a little too much, even for a state as great as Texas.

If you couldn't guess, these guys had a hard-won, well-earned reputation on a conservative Christian campus for being rabble-rousers, troublemakers, ne'er-do-wells, hooligans, or all of the above. And the Sub T-16 frat guys preened like peacocks about their exploits. They were proud to be the bad boys of ACU.

So you can imagine my shock when those four guys in that pizza parlor started talking to me.

"Todd! We're so sorry! We didn't know it was you that we flipped off!"

I couldn't believe what I was hearing. *They're sorry?* What an amazing answer to a funny prayer.

I paused and smiled before I replied. "I'm not sorry. I've been wanting to meet you guys for a long time. In fact, I've been praying for you and your friends in your fraternity."

Now it was time for their jaws to drop in shock. The looks on their faces spoke volumes about their expectations of how I'd handle that situation.

I think most people might have either said nothing at all or would have simply said, "No problem," and gone on their way. A few would have still been angry about being flipped off. But I believe I was able to answer calmly and with full sincerity for one reason: I'd once been a Sub T-16 kind of guy, too.

Before seeking my undergraduate degree at Oklahoma University, I didn't know God. I was a hoodlum, too. I'd go to bars for all the wrong reasons. I lived to portray an image God did not create me for. Missing out on God's love, I'd run to any temporary, rebellious fulfillment just to escape from the pain of dealing with my weaknesses and what others thought of me. I was a rolling rebel and a sinner in need of saving; but no one had told me that then.

Thankfully, praise God, he placed a mentor in my life who kept knocking on my dorm room door and led me back to Christ. He spoke into me who I am in Christ, which is night and day compared to how I saw myself. In thinking about how similar I once was to the men who sat before me in the pizza parlor, I told myself, *Everything that people say on campus about these guys is exactly what Jesus saved me from at my weakest points in my spiritual life when I was at OU. How can I deny them the same love and acceptance Christ has shown me?*

I sat with them, dined with them, and talked with them. Before my eyes and over a few slices of pepperoni, I saw God break walls down.

Rolling through the Doors God Opened

A few weeks later, I felt a tap on my shoulder during a worship service.

"Todd, my name is Michael. I am the president of the Sub T-16 frat. I heard you met some of our guys. We'd like you to come speak to our fraternity at one of our meetings. We never do this—have people come share who aren't in the fraternity, no less share about Jesus with us—but we heard what you did with the guys at the pizza place."

I smiled. "Of course!" But I was also thinking, *Lord, I don't know what you're doing, but this is cool, and I look forward to seeing what you'll do next.* Christ, whose power flows through my weakness, made a door through a barrier that no human strength could construct.

> Christ, whose power flows through my weakness, made a door through a barrier that no human strength could construct.

When I arrived at the meeting, I was faced with a roomful of guys all holding cups. I didn't understand why until one of them spat into his. Then, almost as if on cue, all the other guys did the same in quick succession. They were spitting dip so loudly that I couldn't decide if it was a horrendous noise or a melodic rock song. I wondered if I'd be able to talk over them, or if they'd even listen to this guy with a speech impediment.

But as soon as I began speaking, the room went quiet. I didn't hear even one spit.

With my labored speech, I told them what God had once revealed to me. I shared more than this, but the gist was simple: "You are pure men of God . . . covered by the blood of Jesus. Before someone came into my life and told me that the Lord loves me and wants to use me in my weaknesses, spiritually and physically, I was doing the same kinds of things you are. But God is in the business of changing hearts. If you believe in him, you are pure, cleansed men of God."

Then I spat on the ground for effect.

Just kidding.

I waited, unsure of what to expect from such a direct teaching to a roomful of tough frat guys. But what I saw and heard next floored me: they stood up and clapped for a good minute. Then, they formed a line next to me. Nearly every man said something like, "Thank you so much. You don't know what you did for me tonight." Then each of these "tough" guys let me give them a big ol' hug.

I experienced those invisible walls being broken down again. I saw the cross creating a bridge from lostness to salvation. I witnessed Jesus using my weakness yet again to help others realize their strength: who they truly are in Christ! I saw how Jesus lifts up the spiritually weak, those who don't think they have anything worth giving to God.

My physical weakness connected with their spiritual weakness and barriers were destroyed: barriers between them and me, and, more impacting, barriers between them and God. When I think back to that talk I gave to those frat guys, I'm glad Jesus wanted to be with me in my weakest moment so he could lift them up in their weakest moments.

Later that night, I rolled to my apartment. As soon as I entered, I saw both of my roommates with their jaws dropped. "Todd, there are some guys in your bedroom." With almost fearful faces, they added, "Sub T guys!"

I didn't know what to make of that kind of statement, so I slowed my roll into my bedroom. I saw three Sub T-16 guys about to leave; but just beyond them, I saw my bed—covered with frat shirts, sweatshirts, and caps.

After the guys had left, I saw the note they'd left too: "To the new honorary Sub T, you do not realize what you've done for us tonight. Thank you so much."

What?! What love they showed me to honor me as one of their own! At that moment, in their apparent spiritual weakness and my physical weakness, they'd given me the love of Jesus. Weaknesses were becoming strengths. Walls and barriers were crumbling.

I wore one of the Sub T-16 sweatshirts the next day, and the looks I received from others were, well, interesting. Some just said, "Cool sweatshirt, Todd!" The other Sub T guys gave me high fives. But some people whispered, "Todd, why are you wearing that sweatshirt? Don't you know about them?" To which I would silently reply, *I* do *know about them.* And I'd loudly reply, "I'm . . . haaaappy . . . to know them! They're my friends!"

I wanted to tell these whispering worriers that the Sub T guys just needed someone to speak identity into their lives. They needed to be reminded of who they are and, more so, *whose* they are. When weakness breaks down walls, it sometimes takes a little while for others to recognize the breach.

God Destroys Human-Made Barriers

In a chapel speech I gave in front of thousands, with Sub T-16 members sitting in the front row with eyes open (and not in the back row spitting), I shared with the entire ACU student body that *we* were harlots whom Jesus had died for and made clean, breaking every barrier between humans.

I asked, "What if God had told a godly man to marry a prostitute?" I answered myself, "He did! He told Hosea, a man after God's heart, to marry Gomer, a harlot. This depicts the good news of Jesus! God turned dirty, weak, sinful beings into his spotless bride through the blood of his son's weakened body on the cross!"

I ended the speech with, "*You* were weak whores. *I* was a weak whore. But we are *all* saved and cleansed by the blood of Jesus's weak body!"

God obliterates barriers between "good" and "bad" people. He uses perceived weaknesses to destroy human-made barriers.

And nowhere was the barrier-breaking more evident to me than where the Sub T guys sat during that chapel message. For as long as I could remember, they'd sit in the back row of the balcony of our mandatory chapel meetings, just a-spittin' and a-dippin' in rhythm to *How Great Thou Art*. But on that day, these renewed men of God sat on the front row.

And I don't think they spit even once.

A decade later, I ran into the frat guy who'd first flipped me off. I learned that, by that time, he'd grown into a strong, thriving man of God with a Christ-centered family. By letting Jesus use my weakness to break the barriers that had been blocking the Sub T men from lives of Christian freedom, their lives had changed— because those men finally realized whose they were.

All that had been required of me was an openness to those most would deem "other."

Like Paul said, "There is no distinction between Greek and Jew" (Col. 3:11). At the time, I didn't know anyone who was as "Greek" as the Sub T frat guys. As God used Paul, the man who boasted in his weaknesses, to transcend stereotypes and reach the Greeks (whom the Jews deemed as "other"), I experienced God using my weakness to break down the walls of stereotypes.

God did this first though: he had all the power in the universe yet became weak on the cross to break down barriers and walls of all stereotypes so we can see each other with the eyes of Jesus.

Weakness Breaks Down Cultural Barriers

Do you know the Portuguese word for *wheelchair*? I don't either, nor did the translator in Brazil.

In fact, I don't know any Portuguese, but I didn't let that stop me from traveling to Rio de Janeiro to support my spiritual mentor from my days at the University of Oklahoma. As I've shared, I was frustrated with my job search after grad school. Consequently, I chose to make the best of a bad situation and leave the country! I decided to travel the world to share and show how God's power is displayed through our weaknesses. Rio seemed like a great first destination—except for two important facts:

1. English is not their first language, and it's hardly their second.
2. Wheelchair accessibility (e.g., ramps, sidewalks, and bathroom rails) was a foreign concept.

So, I rolled onto the airplane by myself, walked the aisles while holding onto the seats, then sat in my seat to fly to a country where I only knew two people, where I couldn't speak one word of the language, and where I'd have an even harder time of getting around than usual. As soon as I disembarked from the plane, I realized: *these barriers seem bigger than me.*

I preached at the church there nightly. At that time, I was preaching more in a Portuguese church than I'd ever done in an English-speaking church. I began sharing about my weakness and how I was thankful for my cerebral palsy. I'm pretty sure the interpreter stumbled when looking for the Portuguese equivalent of *wheelchair*, but how would I really know?

Every afternoon, the town's residents would meet me to walk the city streets as I shared the good news of Jesus. I thought, *I have to pull teeth to get people to do this with me at home. This is great!* Every day, at least two locals would walk with me. I'd stop to meet people most would overlook. My new Brazilian friends would translate for me. The one Brazilian friend who interpreted for me held on to every slow word I got out. I witnessed more barriers collapsing, both between my Brazilian friends and me (the foreigner), as well as between my Brazilian friends and the people on the streets whom they may have never considered speaking to before.

I thought about how ironic it was that most of the people there couldn't understand me, yet it wasn't due to my speech impediment. And even despite our language differences, we became close friends during those few days.

At one point, the pastor of the church we were helping told me that a certain family wanted me to stay with them. "Todd, they speak absolutely no English, and I know you speak no Portuguese. We'll understand if you don't want to go."

I didn't hesitate with my answer. "Game on! I want to do it!"

The drive to their modest home was . . . bumpy. Brazilian cars aren't meant to hold wheelchairs, and brazen drivers only yield to the loudest of horns. Still, we arrived, and I had the *best* authentic Brazilian meal ever. The children there felt like my siblings. One even spoke a few words of English. Through that child, I discovered that the family wanted to take me to a special place. Always up for adventure, I wondered where we might be going.

Later, we traveled to the middle of the city, and I found myself facing a massive wall of a hundred steps or more. I got out of my wheelchair, and the family took hold of both of my arms. Together, we ascended.

It was the hardest stair master workout I've ever done.

Even though my legs pulsed with pain, I felt Christ's love pulsating through this Christian community. They were my literal strength, helping me accomplish something I could never have done on my own. We were bonding on a deep, heart level as their strength complemented my weakness.

By the time we made it to the top, I was exhausted beyond belief. My legs alternated between numbness and deep pain. But then I looked out upon the deck. The mystery of where they wanted to take me revealed itself in splendor and glory.

Arms wide and with his head slightly bowed, the *Cristo Redentor* statue loomed over us.

Better known in the States as the "Christ the Redeemer" statue, it's the ninety-eight-foot-tall statue of Jesus you've likely seen. It's a famous landmark in Rio that's a tourist destination for a reason. The statue is impressive, especially as we saw it: lit up so brightly over the whole city.

But what was impressed upon me at that moment was the fact of Jesus's decision to make himself weak and die on that cross so that barriers of all kinds could be broken, just like the ones that had fallen between this slurring English speaker and his new Brazilian friends. Seeing Jesus's arms outstretched over the city, these words came alive:

> After these things I looked, and behold, a great multitude which no one could count, from every nation and all tribes and peoples and tongues, standing before the throne and before the Lamb, clothed in white robes, and palm branches were in their hands; and they cry out with a loud voice, saying, "Salvation to our God who sits on the throne, and to the Lamb." (Rev. 7:9–10)

I was so elated that I don't remember much about our return trip. But I do remember that I never felt so restful and peaceful as I did when we were back in that family's home. And just when I thought my day of being treated like royalty was over—because I was given an opportunity to witness the kingdom of God like I never had before—the father in the home came into my room with a small plate of cookies and milk. As he strummed his Brazilian guitar, he sang a sweet lullaby to me. The next thing I knew, I was awake the next morning, praising God for the power of his weakness on the cross to destroy barriers of all types.

My Haitian Musical

Early on in my spiritual quest to see how much of God's power I could experience and display in my weaknesses, I stepped off a twin-engine plane and onto my wheelchair in a different land devoid of sidewalks and ramps. The potholes in the so-called roads of Cap-Haïtien, Haiti, were too deep for cars to travel over, and much less a wheelchair. So, hoisted up by friends, I was placed into the back of a dump truck. We rode through rivers and over rough terrain. I bounced and rolled so much I thought I was going to fly out of the dump truck with every bounce.

Eventually, we arrived in a small village called Benjamine, where we worshiped with a church and went to the minister's house for dinner. Well, *house* is exaggerating. About the only thing I saw in their hut was a long table overflowing with food, given out of generosity despite their poverty. They may have been lacking, but they had everything.

I also saw ten children playing outside of the minister's house, who I think weren't sure what to think of me. Because I couldn't speak Creole, I quickly learned a song as popular as "Amazing Grace" in their language. After dinner, I rolled out of the family's house into the midst of the children. All I knew to do was sing that song. The lyrics declared "Oh, won't you take me to my Father's House, where there's joy, joy, joy!"

I didn't realize they'd take me literally!

They started pushing my wheelchair around the hut and through the garden and flowerbed. They were too caught up in the moment to think of details like flowers. Then they pushed me onto the main road. I was shocked and excited, but I didn't understand what was happening. Suddenly, I noticed more and more children coming along, maybe even fifty in all, singing and dancing in worship, and all pushing me through the middle of the small village road. It was very surreal!

My missions team watched in awe. I was thrilled by the experience and reveled in that moment of true worship through song and dance. I could never have dreamed of something like that happening to me. Growing up, my speech pathologist had always told me, "Todd, when you sing your words, you do not stutter." But life is not a musical, so I always refrained from singing. But this instance of my life was a musical. I was on a journey beyond myself because God had broken down a language barrier with my speech impediment through the singing of a simple song.

It was then that I knew I wanted more of that kind of life—one that has nothing to do with me and will be gladly caught up in God's power perfected in my weaknesses, breaking into my calling to break down every wall. I wanted to be a barrier-breaker for all the barriers Christ had broken down for me.

Like Paul said in Colossians 3:11, "There is no distinction between . . . barbarian, Scythian." To me, traveling to Rio and Haiti seemed barbaric, because I wasn't afforded some of the niceties to which I'd become accustomed, like wheelchair ramps and ease-of-access. And, as Haiti is one of the poorest countries in the West, it suffers from a type of "barbarism" caused by economic weakness: extreme poverty. But God asks us to make no distinction between "us" and "them" because "Christ is all, and in all."

Weakness Breaks Down Hostile Barriers

Through my travels and so many other circumstances in my life, I began to realize that *we are all weak*. When you share your story of weakness with others, it helps them embrace their weakness and see the truth that it can become their strength.

Nowhere has this been more apparent to me than during a heated "discussion" at a church's Town Hall meeting. I call it a "discussion" because it was more a public airing of complaints against church leadership. In fact, the church's Town Hall meeting resembled a secular government meeting.

Even though I'd only been visiting the church for a few weeks, I knew that its members were fearful of another impending church split. I guess they had reason to feel that way: in five years, they'd suffered two church splits. It was little wonder that this Town Hall meeting seemed filled with so much anger and frustration.

As the meeting began, members would walk up to the mic in the middle of the aisle and tell their side of the issue. They'd loudly complain about what they felt wasn't going right within their church. This would, in turn, cause more members to feel anger. The room temperature seemed to rise, but I'm pretty sure no heater had kicked on.

Then, to make matters even less Christlike, one member was so upset over the church's current state of affairs that he asked the leadership to step outside of the auditorium so that he (and the other members, ostensibly) could freely talk about the leaders without their presence.

Is this a healthy church or an unspiritual, verbal, ultimate fighting match? Barriers between people were becoming more vivid than the walls surrounding us.

After the church's leaders stepped outside of the auditorium, more insults and complaints echoed through the microphone one by one. It saddened me. Then the Holy Spirit whispered into my ear, "Go to the microphone."

Do what?! I'm new to this community.

I hesitated because I didn't know what to say. Even as I rolled to the microphone, I didn't know what to do. I felt like people were looking at me and thinking, *What is he doing there?* I was sure they'd soon think, *What is this speech-impaired guy in a wheelchair going to say?*

They weren't even listening to one another. Would they listen to my impeded words? Maybe they weren't needed at all. I remembered the apostle Paul's words: "For the Kingdom of God is not a lot of talk; it is living by God's power" (1 Cor. 4:20 NLT).

So I didn't speak. Rather, I got out of my wheelchair and onto my knees.

Everyone witnessed a weak man making himself weaker. Then I said what I knew, and I said it to the only one who could really do anything about the church's situation: "God, we are weak. We cannot figure this out. We need you. We need the love that Jesus, in his weakness, displayed on the cross. Heal this church. Destroy the barriers. Make us one."

A noise suddenly rolled throughout the auditorium. I glanced up to see what was happening. It seemed that everyone in the room had gotten onto their knees as well. They turned from making their strong opinions to taking a weak position on their knees, where God's power could show up the most.

Again, without a doubt, I saw the Lord break down human-constructed barriers through the celebration of weakness. With my Christian brothers and sisters praying along, I finished my prayer for this community: "Lord, we are weak. We don't know what to do. We pray for your will to be done on earth as it is in heaven. In Jesus's name, Amen."

After that, people no longer approached the mic to gripe; rather, they prayed. After fifteen minutes, someone remembered: "Hey, let's invite our leaders back into the room!" Then someone else offered, "Let's pray over our leaders, that the Lord would bless them." Soon enough, the church was praying over the leaders whom they'd just asked to leave.

I was amazed at God's movement in that time. I realized that the catalyzing change at that Town Hall meeting occurred through a weak vessel—me—choosing to make himself weaker by getting onto his knees and crying out for God's help. When you let yourself become weaker, others let themselves be weak, then walls break.

> When you let yourself become weaker, others let themselves be weak, then walls break.

Weakness to the Rescue

To many, what I did at that Town Hall meeting may have seemed fearless. To speak *that way* in front of so many people at a church I'd hardly attended? To proclaim God's truth, that he wanted a united church of weaklings, in front of people who wanted "their side" to win? When we lead boldly displaying our greatest weaknesses, dividing walls crumble.

That wasn't the only time God used me in that way.

All who know me know that my passion is to spread the love of Jesus far outside of the church walls to those who do not have faith. For my first job after seminary, as you know, I was a campus ministry intern at Louisiana State University. I spent a lot of time meeting students at the bar strip on Chimes Street. I also spent a lot of time sweating. If you've never been there, being down on the bayou and far too close to swampland makes every day feel like you're in a sauna—except there's no door to escape.

At one time, LSU had been known as America's top party school. When I was there, I was pretty sure it was still in the running.

One night, as I rolled down the same street I'd rolled down before, meeting students to share hope, I saw a guy who may have been getting into trouble, or at least thinking about it. I heard a loud male voice and a young woman's stressed response. I rolled toward the noise, hoping to bring peace to bear on hostility.

The guy had muscles on his muscles. I could tell that the blonde woman he was with was trying to flee, but he wouldn't let her. Without a word, I rolled up to the couple. The angry, persuasive young man was trying to get the young lady into his car. I reached my hand out to stop him, and then we began talking.

I realized they'd just met. Ashley didn't want to be there. She needed help. But the man didn't want to let her go. (He needed help in a different way.) As he became increasingly upset about my intrusion into what he had hoped his night would entail, I simply said, as loudly, clearly, and confidently as I could, "It's time for her and me to go now."

Thankfully, he relented.

Without a word, Ashley walked alongside me until we reached a crowded, lit area. Then, she thanked me.

I replied, "Thank you for what?"

"I think I would've been raped or worse if you hadn't come along." She looked up and down at my wheelchair. Maybe it was just then registering with her what kind of guy had helped her. "Why did you get involved in that scary situation? And how did you calm that guy down? Most guys would have looked at that large man and walked by and not cared!"

I smiled and asked the question I'd asked hundreds of people before: "Do you know Jesus?"

Startled, Ashley hesitated then replied, "I used to go to church, but not anymore."

As I'd done with so many others, I repeated my question: "But do you know Jesus?"

She didn't know how to reply. Well, her silence was reply enough.

And where there's silence, especially Jesus-led silence, Todd Lollar isn't afraid to speak.

In so many words—probably in too many words—I said, "I love Jesus, which means I'm called to be a peacemaker. Jesus said, 'Blessed are the peacemakers, for they will be called children of God.' Jesus is a peacemaker too. He breaks down *every* barrier that the world tries to build up. The apostle Paul was talking about Jesus when he wrote, 'For he himself is our peace, who has made us both one and has broken down in his flesh the dividing wall of hostility.' And I don't have to fear man because God is with me. Jesus makes me bold and strong in my weakness."

I said goodbye and reminded her that God was with her. I didn't know what happened after that—until five years later.

During that time of joblessness, I received a letter in the mail from some woman I didn't recognize. But as soon as I began reading the letter, I remembered: Ashley in Baton Rouge! She thanked me for physically and spiritually saving her. She told me about her first mission trip she was about to take. I was in awe of God's mysterious ways. To this day, I still have no idea how she found me or got my address, especially before social media existed!

Her letter was a means of grace to me at that time. Her words reminded me that the same awesome God who'd broken down barriers through my weakness to save Ashley's life on that night so long ago is the same God who would break down the barriers of employment discrimination due to my weaknesses I was facing at the time.

The Divine Power of Weakness

I've seen how God uses weakness to break down the walls of stereotypes, the barriers of culture, and the defenses of hostility. The kingdom of God isn't like the stereotypes we held to in high school, where something as shallow as clothing often defines people groups. The strong jocks wear the athletic clothes. The weak nerds wear glasses. The cool kids wear the latest trends. The poor kids make do with hand-me-downs.

> How awesome it is that divine power travels through your weakness to break down every barrier between people in your life!

Rather, you and I, we're *all* weak in God's kingdom. No barrier, no dividing wall is too strong for God to dismantle in your life. "For though we live in the world, we do not wage war as the world does. The weapons we fight with are not the weapons of the world. On the contrary, they have divine power to demolish strongholds" (2 Cor. 10:3–4 NIV). How awesome it is that divine power travels through your weakness to break down every barrier between people in your life!

If you allow him, God will use your weakness to expand his reign.

If we'd all allow him to be our strength, he can break down *every* barrier we've built up.

And what a world that would be, filled with walls breaking down as you transparently live life in God's power through your weaknesses!

CHAPTER 7

TODAY'S WEAKNESS IS TOMORROW'S ENCOURAGEMENT

"And let us consider how we may spur one another on toward love and good deeds."

—Hebrews 10:24 NIV

Your weakness doesn't have to be disabling.

I know. That's a little ironic coming from a guy whom some people would label "crippled"; but it's true: even a weakness, any weakness, that has crippled you can be used by God to strengthen you and encourage others. Out of the courage you have from God's power flowing through your weakness, you can encourage others to likewise live *in courage* through God's power flowing through *their* weaknesses.

For all my life, other people have often defined me by what they see and hear. They see a man in a wheelchair and hear my speech disfluency. Words get elongated, and I don't talk as quickly as most people. Others often have to work at listening to me. I've seen this put people off.

In fact, when I was in seminary, I told a professor of my intentions to seek a master of science in biblical and related studies. Without a hint of sarcasm, he flatly said, "You'll never get your master's." Although I don't know his reasons for saying that, I assume he saw my exterior and judged as the world often does. Maybe he thought the work would be too overwhelming. Maybe he thought I'd turn a one-hour preaching class into two hours. Maybe he didn't know I'd mastered using fewer yet more impactful words to compensate.

His words of death almost killed me, but I knew that such discouragement, which is often based on outer appearances, was not from God. I knew that God's calling on my life was stronger than the "words of death" others might toss my way. I knew that the Holy Spirit's power would help me achieve my God-given calling and that he would always help me discern the good words from the bad. I've since learned a discipline for living a victorious life, which is to hear words of life from God over the words of death from a human.

I received my master's degree three years later, but the inner pain of that professor's blunt denial of my dreams required time to heal. Through his louder, more loving voice, God reminded me: when God gives you a vision of embracing his power through your weakness, provision follows.

I Have Never Been Eloquent

While attending the University of Oklahoma (Boomer Sooner!), I began speaking and teaching small groups at the request of a campus minister who'd been showing me the ways of Jesus. I was scared to do so at first. I didn't know at this point that speaking or preaching would be a calling of mine. I figured my speech impediment would be a literal impediment for anyone listening.

So, after finishing what seemed to be a tragic, devastating teaching session, I wheeled back to my dorm room and wondered if anyone had gotten anything from what I had just shared, because I had stuttered *all* the way through my talk! I prayed that they did, but I felt like a fake. I questioned what I felt as a calling into full-time ministry. I thought, *What right do I have to think that God could use someone like me, a stutterer and a slurrer, to speak and teach others?*

Gratefully, God didn't allow me to be discouraged and wallow in self-pity for very long. Brad Brickell, a good friend of mine in college (and still today), spoke just a few simple words into me: "Todd, you're a gifted speaker."

I was floored by his encouragement!

Back then, maybe because I hadn't been a public speaker for long, my speech impediment was very prominent. Maybe Brad was just being nice, but I knew better. Because of our friendship, I knew Brad wasn't just telling me what I wanted to hear. If he had thought I *wasn't* a gifted speaker, he probably wouldn't have said anything. But he had been purposefully specific with his encouragement, and God knew that's what I needed to hear at that precise moment. Through Brad's encouragement and what seemed to have been an embarrassing incident, God showed me that public speaking would be one of my callings.

Although I'd received timely words from a friend, which we all need more than we think we do, the deeper and longer-lasting encouragement came as a result of my daily quiet time. As God would have it, I was reading through the Bible in a year, and I just so happened to be reading the early part of Exodus at that time, where God gives Moses a God-sized mission to be his spokesperson.

When God told Moses to confront Pharaoh about the Israelites' hard labor and to lead and free them from bondage in

Egypt, Moses replied, "Pardon your servant, Lord. I have never been eloquent, neither in the past nor since you have spoken to your servant. I am slow of speech and tongue" (Exod. 4:10 NIV).

I couldn't help but see myself mirrored in Moses's excuses:

- "I have never been eloquent." Check!
- "Neither in the past nor since you have spoken to your servant." Check!
- "I am slow of speech and tongue." Double check!

I thought, *That's me! I'm* that *Moses! I'm slow of speech!* This is the way Todd Lollar speaks! I was floored with encouragement. I saw my weak self in God's metanarrative! God invites us, with weaknesses and all, into his grand story. This is not new. God has always encouraged weak people to do big tasks by his strength! (And I saw how anyone's story can always be found in God's metanarrative.)

Then, through his Word in a very special daily quiet time, God spoke the words of encouragement I needed to hear: "The LORD said to [Moses], 'Who gave human beings their mouths? Who makes them deaf or mute? Who gives them sight or makes them blind? Is it not I, the Lord? Now go; I will help you speak and will teach you what to say'" (Exod. 4:11–12 NIV).

In a flash, I realized that God had used the poor public speaker *with a speech impediment* to part the Red Sea, one of God's most incredible miracles. Because Moses had faith in God, believed that what he said was true (even while knowing his own weaknesses), and boldly proclaimed God's truth, God used him. Wow!

Can God's words of life that moved weak people in the Bible move us to live in courage for God too? The answer is an emphatic yes! God *gave* me my mouth! This was no mistake. God will do the same through my speech impediment for his glory.

I thought, *I want to be* that *Moses, that kind of man of God, that kind of spokesman for God!*

Years later, I told my friend, Dr. Seamster, this story of how God had encouraged me about my speech impediment. Dr. Seamster shed new light on this experience and encouraged me that Aaron, Moses's older brother and the one whom God picked to speak in Moses's place, *never* actually spoke for Moses. Moses was his own spokesman. God may have given Aaron to Moses for mere encouragement, but that's how *powerful* encouragement can be! Encouragement empowers us to live in courage with our weaknesses.

> Encouragement empowers us to live in courage with our weaknesses.

God also used a non-native English speaker to further reveal how he would choose to encourage others through my speech disfluency. During my first ministry internship post-seminary, at Louisiana State University, I met an international student. After many conversations together, she told me, "Todd, I like the way you talk."

I paused for what must have been an eternity as loud thoughts banged around my head: *Do what? I've never heard that before! Why in the world would anyone like the way I talk?*

She must have known what I was thinking because she answered the question I couldn't get to come out of my mouth. "I'm learning the basics of English. Students here speak English so quickly that I cannot understand them. But I enjoy communicating with you because I can keep up with the pace of your speech!"

I smiled from ear to ear.

What a word of unexpected and purposeful encouragement! I learned then what I'll never forget: your weaknesses can encourage others and meet them where they're at—often in ways you wouldn't even expect. In this case, she needed a friend to talk slowly. I needed someone to give me courage that there is a purpose for my weak speech.

Since college, I've been blessed to speak to groups around the world, in universities and giant churches, and in countries like Haiti and Brazil. When I speak in front of thousands, afterward, I'll often hear that people were so quiet in holding on to my every word, you could hear a pin drop. My response? "I'm always dropping something. I hope they didn't hear *that*."

The words that have come out of my mouth attest to the truth of 1 Corinthians 2:3–5: "I was with you in weakness and in fear and in much trembling, and my message and my preaching were not in persuasive words of wisdom, but in demonstration of the Spirit and of power, so that your faith would not rest on the wisdom of men, but on the power of God." Hearts long for encouragement, and weak vessels seem to produce stronger encouragement. This kind of weak encouragement inspires others to live life in courage! God's power through your weak words ignites others to be weak vessels of God's power.

Can you guess what my topic always is? It's what I can never stop talking about, and it's the reason this book exists: to encourage people to live courageously for Jesus in their weaknesses. I want to be so known as an encourager that I might as well change my name to Barnabas, whose name means "Son of Encouragement" (Acts 4:36). You can be that source of courage into someone else's weaknesses too!

You Have an Eternal Encourager

Did you know that God provides us with "eternal encouragement"? Just pause for a moment and consider how freeing those two words are.

To help you visualize this, just imagine that you always had a cheerleader in your corner who constantly and genuinely told you how well you were doing at life. I have to imagine that you'd feel like you could accomplish anything. That's how you ought to feel with God in your corner.

God as our eternal encourager comes from 2 Thessalonians 2:16–17: "May our Lord Jesus Christ himself and God our Father, who loved us and *by his grace gave us eternal encouragement* and good hope, encourage your hearts and strengthen you in every good deed and word" (NIV—emphasis mine). That's a stunning string of words. Not only does God mightily encourage you to live a life beyond yourself, but he also gives you strength beyond your apparent weakness!

I prefer to see the word "encourage" as "in courage," because God encourages us to live life "in courage" for Jesus. Even though I'm pretty well practiced at talking to others about Jesus, I still need to be "in couraged" by Christ every time he prompts me by his Spirit to talk to someone new about him. And every time I obey, he provides the courage I need in order to give encouragement that the recipient desperately needs.

In fact, when I'm at a store, in a coffee shop, or wherever, my heart will be pricked to encourage someone. But I don't know them and I don't even know what they need to be encouraged for. When I joyfully follow through and act on this prompt, God's Spirit in me gives me the strength and the words that person needs!

Why does it work that way? Why does courage often follow encouragement? Think back to the cheerleader example, but make it more personal this time. When was the last time someone spoke a word of encouragement into your life that acknowledged your deepest passions and skills and gave you a vision of how to use those to the fullest to impact the world for God?

The encourager pulls a mask off you that you're clinging to so tightly for fear that you'd be truly known. But once your gifts and talents are proclaimed, you feel lifted up, appreciated—loved. In seeing you for who you really are, the encouragement you receive inspires you to believe you're able to be who you were created to be, the person you'd always felt like you *should* be. You accepted their encouragement and felt the courage in the midst of your weaknesses to pursue what they'd just named your calling.

Now magnify that feeling times infinity.

If God names and proclaims your gift, he's effectively saying, "This is my beloved child in whom I am well-pleased." Notice: when God said those words to his Son, Jesus, he was encouraging Jesus *before* Jesus accomplished most of the amazing miracles in his ministry! God is pleased with you and you alone—not with what you can or cannot do, not by your strengths or your weaknesses, but by who you are, your identity in him. With such encouragement, we live and operate from that identity, weaknesses and all! If he encourages the most hidden recesses of your heart, how will you *not* feel as courageous as a lion?

That's why encouragement always leads to courage.

And what's even more amazing is that God asks us to join with him in encouraging others in the midst of their weaknesses for their good and his glory. God does not only ask us to join him in encouraging, but he also speaks for us. When the disciples were concerned about how they'd encourage people with the good news, Jesus encouraged those weak vessels with the truth that they have a supernatural encourager within them to encourage and spark other weak vessels: "For the Holy Spirit will teach you at that time what needs to be said" (Luke 12:12 NLT). Your words can ignite power in your family's and friends' lives. The Holy Spirit is your spokesman when you do not have adequate words. His conduit of encouragement is your weak mouth.

Your Weaknesses Can Encourage Others

I'm a certified life coach. My first client—believe it or not—was a young man who needed help beginning and maintaining his P90X workout routine.

Let me just pause here and remind you: I can't even touch my toes. I'm also in a wheelchair. P90X was not made for guys like me. And yet Chris wanted *me* to coach *him* to achieve his exercise goals, goals I could never reach. I may not be able to do plyometrics, Kenpo, or the ab ripper, but I can encourage.

In fact, a life coach is a type of cheerleader—although I didn't always think of it that way. After earning my master's in biblical and related studies, I couldn't find a job, but people kept encouraging me by telling me I had such an encouraging demeanor. Yet all they were really telling me was, "We don't hire encouragers." I was thoroughly discouraged. To help me make sense of where I needed to employ my calling, I hired a life coach.

With his help, I set three goals for myself that I thought were impossible:

1. Make a higher salary for a future family.
2. Be a husband.
3. Be a dad.

In less than a year, I hit my salary goal *and* got married. A year after that, we had our son, Oliver; and three years later, our daughter, Alifaire—two joys of my life. In thinking about how my life coach helped me achieve those goals, I came to the blunt realization that all he was really doing was *encouraging* me in very practical ways.

That's when the lightbulb went off: *Hire* yourself *as a professional encourager. Become a life coach.* So, in addition to my vocation of ministry, I became a life coach. (To be honest, I think the only reason life coaches exist today is because people no longer regularly meet to encourage one another. They've forgotten Hebrews 10:25: "And let us not neglect our meeting together, as some people do, but encourage one another, especially now that the day of his return is drawing near" (NLT).

When Chris asked me if I was ready to coach him, I replied, "Are you ready to check P90X off your goal list?" He responded enthusiastically. He plunged into his workouts. On the days when he didn't want to work out, I'd remind him of his vision for why he'd wanted to do this exercise program: to be healthier and to have more energy.

> When you truly believe that God's power flows through your frailty, you can encourage others beyond your own abilities.

Ninety days later, a leaner, buffer Chris emerged, triumphant in attaining his P90X goals. I felt stronger too.

When you truly believe that God's power flows through your frailty, you can encourage others beyond your own abilities. More than being inspired by a life coach, Chris had the courage to reach his goals because of God's power encouraging him through a weak vessel—me. If a disabled man can be a P90X coach, anything is possible—so long as God's involved.

The Adequacy of Being Inadequate

My wife and I launched a ministry among young professionals in the Dallas-Fort Worth Metroplex in 2014. We did not know what we were doing at first. We knew we were following God's calling on our lives to mobilize individuals' missional living, but beyond that, we might as well have been out to sea in a boat built for two.

In its first year, 110 young professionals came into the ministry. Our boat had gotten bigger, but we felt like we were shoveling water all the time just to stay afloat. We didn't have an infrastructure in place to support these young men and women so that they could be mobilized to thrive in their missional lives among their daily existing spheres of influence—their family, friends, co-workers and strangers they meet daily. God worked through our inadequacies, and we launched Missional Living Communities™ (MLC™), which covered the landscape of the Dallas-Fort Worth Metroplex.

I remember reading 2 Corinthians 3:4–6 in a critical quiet time with Jesus during that season: "Such confidence we have through Christ toward God. Not that we are adequate in ourselves to consider anything as coming from ourselves, but our adequacy is from God, who also made us adequate as servants of a new covenant, not of the letter but of the Spirit; for the letter kills, but the Spirit gives life." After reading that, it was no wonder why I felt inadequate at what we were trying to do. I was trying to do it myself, but my adequacy and assurance come through Christ alone! Realizing that truth in my heart was a game changer in my daily life.

And what's so wonderfully surprising is that God never wastes what he reveals. He used that revelation for my good and his glory by bringing a young woman into our lives who needed the same kind of encouragement we did.

After graduating with a nursing degree, Elizabeth moved to the Metroplex to seek a job in pediatric care. She was hired on to the high-stress environment of an ICU, and she dove into her career as if God had indelibly marked her to take care of his most vulnerable of creations.

We met shortly after her arrival in Dallas and the beginning of her career. Whenever I asked her how I might pray for her, her answer was often the same: "That I'd feel adequate at my job." I can imagine that new nurses, even despite their education and training, might seldom feel adequate in such an environment. This is how most young professionals with whom I meet feel straight out of college in the first job of their career: weak, alone, vulnerable, and insecure.

I was even more surprised by her answer when I asked her to lead one of our new Missional Living Communities™. Elizabeth is a quiet person, which is not a common trait for the leader of an entire community, but I just knew she'd thrive in leading a community. I asked if she would, and she quickly replied with a resounding yes. I was glad, but I also thought, *She has such confidence here, but not at work. Where is the disconnect?*

Then I realized what God was trying to tell me throughout that situation. She needed to hear words of encouragement. She needed me to be what my college friend Brad had been to me.

The next time I met with Elizabeth, I shared the 2 Corinthians passage and Galatians 2:20 with her: "I have been crucified with Christ; and it is no longer I who live, but Christ lives in me; and the life which I now live in the flesh I live by faith in the Son of God, who loved me and gave Himself up for me." I told her about how my wife and I felt so inadequate in launching our ministry. I encouraged her about how I often felt inadequate in a number of areas in my life, but that I could always come back to the glorious truth that "the life I now live in the body, I live by faith in the Son of God." See, life is more about what God can do through our weaknesses rather than what we can or cannot do out of our strengths, because Christ is in us, we are in him, and we operate from his power!

I told her that we're all weak vessels, even the people with "normal" bodies. We're all inadequate. But, praise God, it's our inadequacy that Christ redeems by becoming our adequacy. Because Christ lives in us through faith, he makes us enough for everything that might come our way. Your adequacy doesn't come from yourself, your strengths, or from what you can accomplish;

it comes from Christ, who lives within you, and his power that also dwells within you. His strength is revealed in your weakness.

Through realizing Christ's adequacy within her, Elizabeth began to thrive as an ICU nurse. I seldom heard her adequacy prayer request in the months and years that followed. Her community continued to grow and thrive. I can't take credit for her newfound confidence at work because she is the one who put her faith to action, but I'm grateful to have been a part of her faith story—and all because I once felt as inadequate as she did. God deeply desires for you to be encouraged into experiencing his adequacy through your inadequacy!

Your words can be powerful along with your weaknesses. "Words kill, words give life; they're either poison or fruit—you choose" (Prov. 18:21 MSG). I choose to share the fruit of life-giving words because those words taste sweet upon my lips. Knowing that God's words spoken through me can give life, purpose, and strength to others, even in their weakest moments, fills me with gratitude for being in their lives for just that purpose.

I can't help but encourage others, because my life was irrevocably changed by the encouraging words of the strongest man I've ever known.

Encouragement Sets You Up for Life

I can't fathom my childhood without my stepdad, Joe Bob. His actual name was Gary, but he nicknamed himself "Joe Bob." I gravitated toward calling him that because it was a personal, dad-like name. Because he was a strong man from a small country town, it stuck. He was my Joe Bob for the rest of his life.

Joe Bob was "larger than life" to me—certainly larger and stronger than my little six-year-old mind could comprehend when he entered my and my mother's lives. As a former Marine who'd seen the terrors of the front lines of the Vietnam War, he lifted weights and worked out religiously—and I don't mean twice a year; I mean every other night, like scheduled prayer.

I remember hitting what he called his "beer belly." Because he told me to, I put all my might behind my tiny fist and punched his gut as hard as I could. My hand rebounded with just as much force, and it hurt for hours after that. The retired Marine vet had rock-solid abs (and this was *decades* before P90X).

I don't know why he felt the need to still work out so much, but his strength—even just his appearance as the manliest man I'd ever know—highlighted my deficiencies. It was as if he was in my life to show without a doubt how different and how much weaker I was than everyone else.

In those days, I wasn't in a wheelchair. Rather, I wore heavy metal braces on my legs. Those Jurassic-era, heavy orthopedics were just as ugly and as uncomfortable as young Forrest Gump made them seem. I lived under the constantly unspoken hope, passed down to me from distant relatives, that I'd walk "normal" one day—if I could just stand the terrible braces. To those around me, becoming immobilized in a wheelchair was giving up and giving in to my weakness. This discouragement crippled me more. But, as you know, God would later revolutionize my mind on what weakness is. I endured, but I hated it. I was six. Can you blame me? What six-year-old do you know who will sit still for more than a minute?

But Joe Bob never made me feel different. And he never tried to push me beyond what my body could bear. In fact, he showed me what strength is redeemed for: to help the weak and the help-less. He used his strength for my good.

Because of my legs, Joe Bob would often place me atop his shoulders just about wherever we walked. One of my fondest memories of childhood is the bird's-eye view of Disneyland Joe Bob provided to me. With my braced legs clanging onto his chest with every step he took, Joe Bob walked the length of the Happiest Place on Earth, a place I never thought I would experience as a kid.

I felt incredibly special, as if I were getting to see and explore the park from a perspective that no other little kid could. Joe Bob even took us ten feet away from real live buffaloes. I couldn't believe my fortune, and I certainly forgot about my legs.

But then Joe Bob started running—and running fast. I felt like I was flying. I felt like a cowboy galloping through the frontier on his fastest, most trusted steed. Everything about who I was—all the pain, all the mockery, all the worry—vanished into the air that whipped all around us. His strength blessed my weakness and set me up for life!

As I remember this defining moment, I have tears in my eyes. Maybe—just maybe—Joe Bob had such a deep desire to work out so that I could experience just one day like that.

A Whisper of Encouragement Leads to an Abundant Life in Weakness

In addition to being the strongest, Joe Bob was also one of the most servant-hearted. So, when my family and I learned of his terminal throat cancer diagnosis, we were devastated. How could such a strong man have something like that happen to him? He was my bionic stepdad. He was supposed to be invincible.

Joe Bob only lived for two years following his diagnosis; but in those two years, he gave me another unforgettable memory, one that actually surpasses that phenomenal Disneyland day.

With his once-taut skin now sagging off his bones, Joe Bob walked over to me, bent down, and hugged me. He held onto me like he might have known it would be his last time to do so. I didn't move because I didn't want the hug to end either.

But then this "man's man," this former Marine with rock-hard abs who might as well have been Samson to me, whispered the most incredible words of encouragement into my ear, belabored though they were through his cancer-ridden throat: "Todd ... you are ... more of a man ... than I ever was."

A few days later, right in front of me in our living room, Joe Bob died.

His gentle whisper of encouragement didn't just impact me at that moment, but it was my rite of passage into manhood. It was his way of saying what Jesus's Father spoke into him, "This is my son in whom I am well-pleased." Those words were his passing the torch of his *inner* strength on to me. He knew what I've had to learn and what I long to teach others: true strength lives within, where Christ lives by faith.

This life-defining moment only required a *whisper* of encouragement. God didn't have to shout to get my attention. The way God spoke so clearly yet so quietly through my stepdad reminds me of the same way God encouraged Elijah. You may remember the end of this passage, but focus on the context leading up to it. Look at how many ways God *could* have encouraged Elijah, but chose a drastically different method:

> So He said, "Go forth and stand on the mountain before the LORD." And behold, the LORD was passing by! And a great and strong wind was rending the mountains and breaking in pieces the rocks before the LORD; *but* the LORD *was* not in the wind. And after the wind an earthquake, *but* the LORD *was* not in the earthquake. After the earthquake a fire, *but* the LORD *was* not in the fire; and after the fire a sound of a gentle blowing. (1 Kings 19:11–12)

If God's been quiet in your life lately, the question might not be, "What have I done?" Rather, the question may be, "How closely have I been listening?" If God uses weakness to make us strong, I'm not sure I know of anything weaker than a whisper.

Sometimes all God needs is a whisper to change a life. I know that was true for me. I pray that this book is that powerful whisper to fuel *you* to live an abundant life in and through your weaknesses.

Words of Encouragement Shift a Mind

Joe Bob's simple yet profound encouragement stays with me. He set the stage for me to become the man whom my wife would marry and my son, Oliver, and daughter, Alifaire, and future children would look up to. He opened my eyes to see and my heart to believe that my weaknesses are not a setback; they are for God to use for greatness to honor him!

Whenever I doubt what God has planned for me, whenever I see my weaknesses as a source of shame rather than boastfulness, whenever I fear the reactions of man more than the favor of God, I hear God slowly whisper, in echoes of past encouragement like I heard from my Joe Bob, and in a cadence like I've had all my life: "Todd . . . you're stronger . . . than you know."

When I hear a seminary professor tell me that postgraduate work isn't achievable, I hear, "You're stronger than you know."

When I wonder why I'm an inspirational speaker when I speak so slowly, I hear, "You're stronger than you know."

When I know people only see my cerebral palsy and my wheelchair, I hear, "You're stronger than you know."

When God places a desire within me for a family, I hear, "You're stronger than you know."

When God calls me to ministry that stretches my faith beyond its comfort level, I hear, "You're stronger than you know."

When a life-coaching client wants *me* to coach him in P90X, I hear, "You're stronger than you know."

And when a new nurse in an ICU unit asks for prayers for help in her new career, I have the glad opportunity to encourage her with the simplest of words: "Your insecurities do not define you, because God is strong within your weaknesses."

And when a reader picks up a book about weakness, I get to encourage you by speaking courage into your weaknesses: "You're stronger than you know, and your deepest weaknesses are your greatest strengths," so that when someone comes to you, you can encourage them with the same message.

In God's hands, your weaknesses are strengths, and your words of encouragement could radically inspire a weak life to live life "in courage." So set this book down and call or meet with someone. Encourage them to live life *through* their weaknesses.

CHAPTER 8

LACK IS THE NEW MORE

"And let endurance have its perfect result, so that you may be perfect and complete, lacking in nothing."

—James 1:4

Do you know how to lack faithfully?

That's a strange phrase, I know, but I mean it. Maybe the better way to phrase it is this: Do you know how to be responsible for the little you have? Do you view what you *don't* have as a gift? Do you see what you lack as a detriment or an advantage?

Personally, I long wrestled with my lack of financial resources, my lack of ministry growth, my lack of skills, and my lack of belief. I felt like the father who had brought his convulsing son to Jesus for healing. When Jesus tells the man, "'All things are possible to him who believes.' Immediately the boy's father cried out and said, 'I do believe; help my unbelief'" (Mark 9:23–24). I've always wanted to believe, but even my desire to believe suffers from the weakness of unbelief.

I saw each of these issues as deficiencies I had to somehow overcome by my own merit. If only I worked harder, I could earn more money. If only I could meet the right people, then my career would explode. If only I could speak better, then I could speak to bigger crowds. If only I could *believe* better and more consistently, then God might bless me and my career.

But I had it all backward.

I needed a lesson in God's economics, where faithful lacking equals kingdom abundance. I needed to learn the wild, other-worldly truth of Jesus's words: "Blessed are you who are poor, for yours is the kingdom of God" (Luke 6:20). How could the poor, the ones with weak resources possessing little if not nothing at all, *own* the kingdom of God? It just doesn't make sense in our world so focused on metrics of success, where abundance—more money, more friends, more skills—means achievement.

My physical life needed to catch up with the spiritual truth that God's power flows through my weaknesses, which had transformed my inner being. I did not realize this truth could transform my vocation and economic realities as well. After much disappointment with my career and finances, I needed to learn that God loves using the "lack" of his faithful stewards.

God's Bad Math

I didn't expect to be jobless after earning my bachelor's degree in business administration *and* a master's degree in biblical and related studies. And I certainly didn't expect to endure joblessness for *seven* years, which felt like forever.

During that time, I didn't receive a steady paycheck. All I had was a God-given calling and a vision that he would use my education and experience—some day. When God gives you a vision, he will give you the provisions. In faithful lacking, these provisions might seem small at first, but God adds what is needed.

Fortunately, when I first moved to the Dallas area, Michael Miller, one of my Sub T-16 fraternity friends at ACU, who would later plant the multicampus church UPPERROOM in Dallas, asked a few members of his church family to help me pay for rent and food. I also intermittently earned (very) moderate income through speaking engagements. And generous people who had heard about my ministry and sought to support God's work through my life gave of their money too.

Even though I desperately wanted to find a full-time career, I knew I was called to be a steward of the little provision I had. In fact, during this time, I became debt-free by paying off credit cards and college loans, started a savings account, and eventually moved into my own apartment (with a garage).

I know, I know. The math doesn't work out here. How could jobless me, with few resources, in his own apartment, get to a financial place like that without a stable income?

You know the answer if you've read the book this far: Jesus's power and unmerited favor in unfavorable circumstances. This powerful truth impacts your life far beyond the spiritual and the emotional.

I believe God blessed my decision to give King Jesus a tithe of everything I received. For many churchgoing Christians, a tithe means giving 10 percent. The belief that 10 percent equals "tithing" comes from many Old Testament passages like Genesis 14:20 and Leviticus 27:32: "For every tenth part of herd or flock, whatever passes under the rod, the tenth one shall be holy to the LORD." But, in the New Testament, Paul says, "Each one must do just as he has purposed in his heart, not grudgingly or under compulsion, for God loves a cheerful giver" (2 Cor. 9:7). I realized the truth that 10 percent is the *baseline* for tithing.

If you've never given to your church, to missionaries, or to ministries, or you haven't been consistent, start with 10 percent. But, for me, there was freedom in my finances when I realized that 100 percent of my finances were really God's that he was *letting* me steward. Without much in my bank account, I learned that being a steward of the 100 percent of the little God had entrusted to me equals more later. That's biblical too. In Luke 16:10, Jesus said, "He who is faithful in a very little thing is faithful also in much; and he who is unrighteous in a very little thing is unrighteous also in much." If you lack faithfully, God can trust you to be faithful with wealth.

Soon after I was convinced I needed to give, I was convicted to give *more*. God prompted me to give *20* percent. I also used whatever extra money I had each month to pay off my debt.

Let's review God's bad math here:

- I didn't have a job.
- I paid rent and other necessities.
- I tithed 20 percent of the income I did have.
- I paid off my debt.
- I even drank coffee from local coffee houses a few times.
- And I started *saving* money.

I have a degree in business management, so I know that shouldn't have been possible. But we must always remember: "With God all things are possible" (Matt. 19:26). This kind of math only makes sense in God's kingdom. He even told us about it a long time ago through one of Jesus's parables:

> If you lack faithfully, God can trust you to be faithful with wealth.

And He looked up and saw the rich putting their gifts into the treasury. And He saw a poor widow putting in two small copper coins. And He said, "Truly I say to you, this poor widow put in more than all of them; for they all out of their surplus put into the offering; but she out of her poverty put in all that she had to live on." (Luke 21:1–4)

How can a poor woman's small two cents be worth more than a rich man's abundant treasure? Jesus gave us the answer, and the answer is something only he could have seen and known. The hidden variable in God's math is the human heart. He knew that the poor widow gave out of her weakness; the rich man gave out of his strength. The poor widow gave all she had; the rich man gave what he thought was sufficient. The poor widow put herself into debt by giving; the rich man sacrificed nothing. The poor widow understood God's economics; the rich man didn't have a clue. The adjectives describing the woman and her giving, *poor* and *small*, actually equate to *rich* and *large* in the kingdom of God!

It doesn't make sense to give *more* when you have *less*; but when you realize that Jesus is all the *more* you need, you'll never have *less*. You will always be giving out of your abundance. Strike that. You'll always be giving out of *God's* abundance granted to you for your time on earth.

So why *not* be a consistent, generous, cheerful giver?

Jesus said it best in the middle of the Sermon on the Mount:

> Look at the birds. They don't plant or harvest or store food in barns, for your heavenly Father feeds them. And aren't you far more valuable to him than they are? . . . So don't worry about these things, saying, "What will we eat? What will we drink? What will we wear?" These things dominate the thoughts of unbelievers, but your heavenly Father already knows all your needs. Seek the Kingdom of God above all else, and live righteously, and he will give you everything you need. (Matt. 6:26, 31–33 NLT)

I know. Even when Jesus tells you not to, it's hard *not* to worry about money, particularly when you don't have a steady job. Without that resource, which seems to make the world go round, it can feel impossible to get ahead. And the longer you're without a job or money to make ends meet, the more you may succumb to thinking as the world does.

But I beg you, as one who's been there, learn God's economics and how he provides through deficiency. It won't help your child pass their math test, but I firmly believe it will help you learn how to trust God more each day.

One year after choosing to give 20 percent, I was debt-free and landed my first job in my career and my calling, my dream job at the time. And the hard economics lesson God taught me in the wilderness of poverty stayed with me through the peaks of having a steady paycheck.

> Even our financial "lacking" equates to abundance in the kingdom of God when we give and give cheerfully.

Now I might go to the coffee shop a few times a week!

Often, what's offered to God is multiplied beyond what we can imagine. Even our financial "lacking" equates to abundance in the kingdom of God when we give and give cheerfully.

After experiencing this kind of "bad math" in my finances, I saw God move in our ministry. If I could trust him with my money, couldn't I trust him with our work?

God's Miraculous Multiplication

When my wife and I first arrived in the Dallas-Fort Worth Metroplex to launch a ministry that would mobilize young professionals in their God-given callings, I was discouraged when our first meetings were sparsely attended. I thought, *I'm doing what I've been called to do. Why aren't people showing up?* But before I became too downcast about our low numbers, which hit me harder than my disability ever did, I had to take another lesson in God's upside-down mathematics class. But this time, he wasn't teaching me about money; he was teaching me about something much more important: people.

One of Jesus's most famous miracles occurred soon after he'd commissioned the twelve disciples to start preaching the good news throughout Galilee and its surrounding villages. Because Jesus had been healing people and word was spreading about this miracle-maker, huge throngs of people seemed to find him wherever he went. That's how he wound up with five thousand hungry men—not to mention the unreported numbers of women and children, which may have increased the crowd size to twenty thousand—hanging on to his every word.

In Luke 9, the disciples saw the crowd and desperately told Jesus to send the crowd away so they could find food to eat. But something happens that surprises the twelve disciples and me. It's so telling (and personally convicting) that Jesus's answer to the disciples' subtly selfish complaint is, "You give them something to eat!" I have to imagine that at least one of the disciples looked around at the immense crowd, glanced down at the five loaves of bread and two fish the disciples had brought, did some quick math, and then thought, *This isn't even enough food for the thirteen of us!*

The disciples saw what they lacked before they saw their Provider. They believed the world's math was the only math. They thought they knew the one they followed—until they experienced this incredible miracle and their misconceptions were suddenly obliterated in a sea of people, bread, and fish. Jesus is God in the flesh. This miracle-maker needed no help in feeding the masses. His character is always inviting weak people like us to be involved in his miraculous living. He fed the five thousand through giving the bread to the disciples and invited them into the work of God in feeding the hungry. In Jesus's humility, miraculous multiplication occurred through the weak hands of the disciples.

Jesus multiplies *people* too, that they might continue the expansion of God's kingdom on earth. Look at Jesus's sending out of the twelve disciples (which, may I remind you, happened shortly before the miraculous feeding of the five thousand):

> And [Jesus] called the twelve together, and gave them power and authority over all the demons and to heal diseases. And He sent them out to proclaim the kingdom of God and to perform healing. And He said to them, "Take nothing for your journey, neither a staff, nor a bag, nor bread, nor money; and do not even have two tunics apiece." (Luke 9:1–3)

Jesus blessed and mobilized the twelve disciples to meet and invest in others. What were only twelve faithful Jesus followers in Luke 9:1 became *seventy-two* in Luke 10:1, multiplied by six just a chapter later. Two millennia later, that twelve has become 2.18 *billion* worldwide Christians. Now that's a huge increase (23,333,333,233 percent increase)!

Notice that the multiplying of bread and fish through the hands of disciples happens right before we see the twelve disciples multiply into seventy-two. Through each disciple touching and handing out the multiplying bread, Jesus foreshadows the same kind of multiplication that will happen in Luke 10:1, a direct result of the twelve disciples being with Jesus and being mobilized by Jesus to touch lives in Luke 9:1!

Businesses today would love to see that kind of increase in their bottom lines. But they could never operate based on God's math, because it's so counterintuitive to what we expect. God can take next to nothing and feed a multitude. He can take twelve average Joes and have them help change the world *forever*. And he can multiply the disciple-making ministry of a mobilized-in-a-wheelchair leader with cerebral palsy from zero to 120 in two years.

Once I learned the only tenet of God's math—trust God with your lack—I rested in his unmerited favor when my numbers didn't seem adequate. I experienced how God's power even flows through my weakness of seeing deficient numbers.

God's Ridiculous Subtraction

Famously, nineteenth-century British pastor George Mueller raised money to build orphanages by simply praying for the funds and *not* telling anyone about his plan. In other words, he never asked others for money, but God answered his prayers. By prayer alone, and with minimal information given to others and no solicitation for funding, Mueller experienced God's provision. In time, over ten thousand children benefited from Mueller's faithfulness.[1]

With unswerving belief—as far as we know—he was certain God would provide for this need. Mueller's words speak to his character and his hope in God:

> It is not enough to obtain means for the work of God,
> but that these means should be obtained in God's way.
> To ask unbelievers for means is not God's way. To press
> even believers to give is not God's way; but the duty and
> privilege of being allowed to contribute to the work of
> God should be pointed out, and this should be followed
> up with earnest prayer, believing prayer, and will result
> in the desired end.[2]

Mueller understood that God can work despite any external displays to the contrary. In the Bible, Gideon had to learn this lesson the hard way.

Because "the sons of Israel did what was evil in the sight of the LORD . . . the LORD gave them into the hands of Midian seven years. . . . So Israel was brought very low because of Midian, and the sons of Israel cried to the LORD" (Judg. 6:1, 6).

During this time in Israel's history, the angel of the Lord appears to Gideon, a strong Israelite, and calls him a "valiant warrior" (Judg. 6:12). Then Gideon, who didn't realize God was defining his future identity, speaks bluntly: "O my lord, if the LORD is with us, why then has all this happened to us? And where are all His miracles which our fathers told us about, saying, 'Did not the LORD bring us up from Egypt?' But now the LORD has abandoned us and given us into the hand of Midian" (Judg. 6:13).

Then God delivers a blunt answer that had to have shocked Gideon, who, even though he had strength, still knew his weaknesses well.

> The LORD looked at him and said, "Go in this your strength and deliver Israel from the hand of Midian. Have I not sent you?" [Gideon] said to Him, "O Lord, how shall I deliver Israel? Behold, my family is the least in Manasseh, and I am the youngest in my father's house." But the LORD said to him, "Surely I will be with you, and you shall defeat Midian as one man." (Judg. 6:14–16)

Isn't this such a fascinating exchange?

For God's reply, another translation reads "Go in the strength you have" (Judg. 6:14 NIV). I think Gideon might be thinking to himself, *I can't just go in the weakness I have. Strength is a resource I am very much lacking.* I can very much relate to that! I don't have much physical strength, but I'm strong in other ways, and the longer I've lived and loved Christ, the more I've learned to "go in the strength I have" and *not* the strength I *want* to have. There's a world of difference between those two.

The key to being able to "go in the strength you have" is found in the last part of the angel of the Lord's reply to Gideon: "Surely I will be with you" (v. 16). When we understand God's way rightly, we see that the strength we have is really weakness. And this is really where our strength begins—it's always God's strength through us. The key to living in strength is fervently acknowledging God's presence and that his power is always with you.

God's Accelerating Addition

When I think about how God is our strength in weakness, I see snow-capped mountains. I feel cold wind whipping my face. I breathe in the scent of pine dancing in fresh air. I hear the whoosh of my fellow skiers as they pass by me and I pass by them.

The first time I ever went snow skiing was shortly after I'd earned my bachelor's degree. Seven friends and I chose to celebrate that milestone at the Winter Park Resort in Colorado because they're known for being a great place for wheelchair skiers.

The first time we ascended the slope, I thought, *Todd, you don't know what you're doing. What are you getting yourself into?!* But I didn't let on to my instructor how nervous I was. Without a word of instruction to me, he tied himself behind me to my sled. Then he spoke three words that simultaneously scared and thrilled me: "Okay, Todd. Go!"

Never one to back down from a challenge, I launched myself onto the packed snow.

At this point, while I'm still at the top of my first run, you should probably know two important facts. First, wheelchair skiers sit on a specialized ski that only has one blade at its bottom. Then we use two shortened ski poles to control our balance and our turns. On this contraption, cerebral palsy isn't my only weakness: I'm a six-foot guy in a sled with poles as short as my arms!

Second, the only skiing I'd ever watched was Olympic speed skiing—where they go straight down the hill as fast as they can.

So, I thought that was how you ski. That was my model.

I couldn't believe how fast I was going. Trees whipped by. My face felt like a cartoon with my cheeks two feet behind my ears. My instructor may have said something, but I was having too much fun to hear him. I flew past other skiers. I couldn't believe the rush. My face felt like it was lagging behind me.

Then, a tree appeared.

A big tree.

That was rapidly growing in size and imminent future pain.

I saw myself, cartoon-like, being splattered into the tree.

In a brief moment of clarity seconds away from slamming into that giant aspen, a thought—like my life—flashed before my eyes: *As if having CP and being in a wheelchair isn't bad enough, I'm about to have some* serious *issues if something doesn't happen* real *soon.*

That's when I felt a strong jerk. My beeline approach to the tree had been diverted from behind by my instructor.

As I recomposed myself and realized that now I *just* had CP and a wheelchair to keep dealing with, my "instructor" said, "Todd, you're supposed to take *very wide turns* to slow down! The straighter you ski, the faster you'll go."

Now you tell me! I didn't say that out loud.

The rest of the trip was fantastic. And even though I could have lost a limb or my life or both during my first downhill skiing experience, God accelerates our lack of skills. In other words, where we lack skill, we still get to experience the blessing of the thrill.

In the moments before impact, I was helpless and weak, and my only hope was the instructor behind me. I had to totally depend on him. If it hadn't been for him, I would have slammed into the tree. If it hadn't been for him, I also wouldn't have been able to ski in the first place. If I hadn't let myself be weak in order to try something new, I wouldn't have been able to experience the next three days of skiing down mountains and having the time of my life.

When I think about this story, I remember what Paul says: "You see, at just the right time, when we were still powerless, Christ died for the ungodly" (Rom. 5:6 NIV). "At the right time," the instructor stopped me *to save me* in my weakness. In a much grander way, Jesus died for us "at the right time" to save us in *our* weaknesses.

In our weaknesses, God wants us to enjoy life and have fun.

He also wants to steer us away from crashing.

But for him to be our strength, we have to choose to trust his words.

Just like Gideon did.

After being chosen by God, Gideon is charged by God. God wants Gideon to lead the Israelites against the Midianites. But instead of *adding to* Gideon's strengths, he *takes away*:

> The LORD said to Gideon, "The people who are with you are too many for Me to give Midian into their hands, for Israel would become boastful, saying, 'My own power has delivered me.' Now therefore come, proclaim in the hearing of the people, saying, 'Whoever is afraid and trembling, let him return and depart from Mount Gilead.'" So 22,000 people returned, but 10,000 remained. (Judg. 7:2–3)

Knowing that "might makes right" in the time in which he lived, Gideon must have thought God's plan was outrageous. *You want me to let the scaredy-cats go? We're going to lose over two-thirds of our army?! We're going to get slaughtered.* But we aren't told what Gideon thought. We're just shown that, like a good soldier, he followed his Chief Commanding Officer's orders.

Have you ever felt ill equipped for a task at hand? Then, on the day when that task is finally before you, some major setback occurs, the resources you need are lost, and everything within you shouts, *How will I ever accomplish this?* I would argue that this is often exactly where God wants you. If we could accomplish great things in our own strength, why would we need God? Just as God didn't want his people to become boastful in their own strength, neither does he want us to become the same.

What's crazy about Gideon's story is that God doesn't stop winnowing his army:

> And the LORD said to Gideon, "You shall separate everyone who laps the water with his tongue as a dog laps, as well as everyone who kneels to drink." Now the number of those who lapped, putting their hand to their mouth, was 300 men; but all the rest of the people kneeled to drink water. The LORD said to Gideon, "I will deliver you with the 300 men who lapped and will give the Midianites into your hands; so let all the other people go, each man to his home." (Judg. 7:5–7)

To put this into perspective, God told Gideon to *decrease* his army from 32,000 men to just three hundred. That's a percentage decrease of more than 99 percent! No business today would want to see that on their bottom line. They'd have gone out of business long before getting to that point.

Incredibly, Gideon and his army of three hundred defeat the Midianites. Grateful for their victory, "the men of Israel said to Gideon, 'Rule over us, both you and your son, also your son's son, for you have delivered us from the hand of Midian.' But Gideon said to them, 'I will not rule over you, nor shall my son rule over you; the LORD shall rule over you'" (Judg. 8:22–23).

Because he'd experienced God's rule within his life, Gideon knew that Israel's only chance at success, peace, and well-being was to let God rule them. So, at the very moment he could have rightfully boasted in his own power, he turned down an offer to become more powerful and willingly made himself weak. When he could have basked in the glory of victory, he pointed to the One whom he knew had given him that victory. Gideon understood, as should we, that the victory was God's alone, because God wants his kingdom to prevail.

To experience such victory today, we must realize that God can use very little to do more than we dare imagine. This victory occurred when Jesus depleted himself of the essence of his resource—himself. That's how he established his rule. But first we have to let him be our King. And allowing him to be King means allowing ourselves to become "poor in spirit" (Matt. 5:3). For when we are poor, inadequate in our spirit, we can become rich in the Holy Spirit.

> For when we are poor, inadequate in our spirit, we can become rich in the Holy Spirit.

God's Unequal Equations

I like how the New Living Translation translates "poor in spirit" in Matthew 5:3: "God blesses those who are poor *and realize their need for him*, for the Kingdom of Heaven is theirs" (emphasis mine). Every day, we *must* realize our need for God. We must be able to honestly assess ourselves—to see our weaknesses and our strengths without embellishing either. We must be able to rightly view ourselves in light of both our humanity and the way God sees us. We must learn to empty ourselves *of* ourselves so that Christ may fill us. This happens through God's unequal equations.

Once you begin to grasp how God's economics works, you'll see it again and again throughout the Bible. In the parable of the talents, ten slaves are given ten "minas" or "talents," which were terms of currency measurement in Jesus's day. One talent equals approximately one hundred days' wages; so ten minas equal six hundred days' wages! The modern-day equivalent of *one* talent (equal to sixty minas) is at least $5,800. In other words, a talent is a lot of money.

In this parable that Jesus told, ten slaves are each given ten talents and asked to "Do business with this until I [the nobleman in charge] come back" (Luke 19:13). One slave doubles his investment and earns ten more minas. Another earns five more minas. But a third slave hid what he was given, saying "I was afraid of you, because you are an exacting man; you take up what you did not lay down and reap what you did not sow" (Luke 19:21). The nobleman has a stern rebuke for him:

> "By your own words I will judge you, you worthless slave.
> Did you know that I am an exacting man, taking up
> what I did not lay down and reaping what I did not sow?
> Then why did you not put my money in the bank, and
> having come, I would have collected it with interest?"
> Then he said to the bystanders, "Take the mina away
> from him and give it to the one who has the ten minas."
> (Luke 19:22–24)

Compare that response to what the nobleman told the slave who had doubled his minas: "'Well done, good slave, because you have been faithful in a very little thing, you are to be in authority over ten cities'" (Luke 19:17).

Now, place yourself in the sandals of these men given these highly valuable talents. If you knew that your boss expected a return, would you risk investing his money? Or would you stow it in a savings account and hope his return wouldn't be imminent?

Now, change the context of the story. Instead of talents representing money, let it represent your actual talents—the giftings God has given you. Have you been hiding your gifts, or have you been risking to be vulnerable so that God might use your gifts to expand his kingdom? When you see how God repays those whom he calls, leaning into using your gifts should come more easily. Again, it's about trusting God's economics.

Remember, Jesus said, "Blessed are the poor in spirit, for theirs is the kingdom of heaven" (Matt. 5:3). Poverty of spirit is the pathway for the continuous flow of the richness of the Holy Spirit. We were made to be filled with the Spirit and emptied of ourselves. In fact, Jesus modeled this for us: "For you know the grace of our Lord Jesus Christ, that though He was rich, yet for your sake He became poor, so that you through His poverty might become rich" (2 Cor. 8:9). Now, Paul is not talking here about financial wealth when he says we may become rich. Rather, he's discussing "this gracious work" (2 Cor. 8:7), by which he means sharing the gospel and increasing God's kingdom. When we do that—when we follow God's plan for how this world ought to work—we'll reap in our hearts and souls what he's sown into us. That's when we can be the man given ten minas who makes ten minas more. That's when we can hear King Jesus one day say, "Well done, good and faithful servant" (Matt. 25:23 NIV).

Strangely enough, when we learn to "lack faithfully" and live in full recognition of our weaknesses, God gives us *strength* for the day. Where once we might have felt fear, God replaces it with boldness. In the midst of opposition to the gospel in Jerusalem, the early church prayed,

> "And now, Lord, take note of their threats, and grant that Your bond-servants may speak Your word with all confidence, while You extend Your hand to heal, and signs

and wonders take place through the name of Your holy servant Jesus." And when they had prayed, the place where they had gathered together was shaken, and they were all filled with the Holy Spirit and began to speak the word of God with boldness. (Acts 4:29–31)

I can attest to such "weak boldness." I once rolled by a pool table in a restaurant pub and couldn't help but notice a muscle-bound man sporting a shirt that read *Jesus is never returning*. I wanted to roll on. God's Spirit stopped me and nudged me to go share the hope of Jesus with him. God's Spirit wanted me to experience his Spirit in me beyond my own spirit.

But as often happens when I'm attentive to God's whispers, the man started telling me about his life. His wife had left him. Her dad was a preacher. He didn't want anything to do with Christianity.

As he spoke, the Holy Spirit spoke to me: *Stand up!* (Side note: people are *very* surprised when I stand from my wheelchair, to say the least.) So I stood, and in a loud, loving voice, I told the man, "Jesus loves you!"

The man jumped back, shocked that I was standing, and maybe more shocked that I was declaring Jesus's love for him in a restaurant full of people. Then he complimented me on my boldness, likely knowing that his imposing stature and controversial wardrobe choices often prevented people of faith from even approaching him. I told him what he'd likely already heard before, that we're all sinners in need of God's love, and that Christ died for us while we were still sinners.

Then he asked me how such a weak, disabled man could be so bold.

Gladly, I replied, "My old self wouldn't have done this, but I'm a new creation. Christ

> I may not have much, but God's math favors those who lack.

lives in me. He's freed me. Because of Jesus, I no longer roll in my weak identity. I roll in Jesus's power." In other words, the resources within myself are depleted. Now I live by the power of the main Source!

I have to imagine that the irony of the situation—me in my wheelchair confronting Mr. Big Man—wasn't lost on Mr. Big Man.

I realized then as I do now: I may not have much, but God's math favors those who lack.

Notes

[1] "George Mueller, Orphanages Built by Prayer," Christianity.com, July 16, 2010, http://www.christianity.com/church/church-history/church-history-for -kids/george-mueller-orphanages-built-by-prayer-11634869.html.

[2] Arthur Tappan Pierson, *George Müller of Bristol* (London: James Nisbet and Co., 1899), 440.

CHAPTER 9

WEAKNESS IN COMMUNITY

*"But Moses' hands were heavy. Then they took a stone
and put it under him, and he sat on it; and Aaron and
Hur supported his hands, one on one side and one on the
other. Thus his hands were steady until the sun set."*
—Exodus 17:12

Melinda and Mark had been dating for two years. The other students at their high school knew them to be inseparable. Some of the girls wished they could find a guy like Mark, or at least to have the kind of relationship that Melinda and Mark had. They doted on each other as high school sweethearts do.

But then Melinda's family suffered a tragic car accident. Although they all survived, Melinda's strength in her legs didn't. She'd been paralyzed from the waist down.

Days after the accident, the talk around the school was that Mark was sure to be single in a few months. But Mark stuck by Melinda's side during her many months of rehabilitation. Their classmates were impressed by his faithfulness. Some of the girls fell even more in love with Mark, longing to have any guy care for them the way he cared for Melinda.

Meanwhile, Melinda put on a brave face for Mark and her family and friends, but she was slowly wilting on the inside. Her self-esteem, which had never really been that high (especially when she was by herself), plummeted. She felt sorry for her predicament. Even worse, she'd heard the talk at school and often caught herself thinking, *Mark probably will leave me. Just look at me. What can I do for him now?*

Despite her doubts, she relished her time with Mark. But as the months wore on and prom drew closer, she couldn't help but notice that Mark was changing. It wasn't his character or his love for her; it was his muscles. Melinda thought, *He must be working out . . . so he can get a better date for prom.* She hated thinking that, but she couldn't help it. When she finally went back to school, she noticed how so many of the other girls were ogling Mark now too. This went on for weeks until Melinda couldn't endure her worries any longer, so she confronted Mark.

"I love you, Mark, but I'm paralyzed, not blind. I've seen what's been going on for a long time, but I just haven't wanted to admit it to myself."

Mark was taken aback, but he didn't interrupt.

"You should just go to prom with someone else, someone who can dance with you, someone who can, well, be better for you. Once I accepted that I wouldn't be able to walk again, I started to accept a harder truth: that you'd very likely leave me. So I'm giving you permission so you don't have to feel guilty about breaking up with the paralyzed girl."

"But, Melinda—"

"Don't tell me I'm wrong, Mark. You've been working out! How could I not notice that!? How could I not notice *all* the other girls noticing that too? I could name ten girls who'd say yes to your prom invitation right now!"

Mark smiled at Melinda.

She was hurt and near tears. "Why are you smiling?"

"Melinda, do you love me?"

"Yes? No. I don't know anymore. I have loved you, for a long time. But after all this happened"—Melinda waved at her useless legs dismissively—"everything changed. You changed."

"How did I change?"

"You bulked up! And you didn't even tell me about it. It feels like you've been keeping a secret from me for a while."

"That's because I have."

Now it was Melinda's turn to remain silent.

"I've been working out *for you.*"

"I don't get it."

"For prom."

"For—"

"My secret is your prom surprise. I've been getting stronger so that I can lift you from your wheelchair, carry you onto the dance floor, and dance with you."

Dancing in Weakness

In this modern-day allegory, it should be easy to tell who stands in for God and who stands in for us. Mark's actions reveal God's unending, unyielding, unconditional love for us in our weakness. Melinda's accusations represent our doubt of that love that stems from the insecurities about our weaknesses we bring into relationships. Her paralysis stands in for any of our shortcomings in our lives. Mark represents God's strength being shown through our weakness.

The dance is our ongoing relationship with God. But the key to dancing is that one partner has to let themselves be vulnerable and weak. They willingly have to take on the role of follower. They must allow the other person to lead. They must choose weakness.

Since you are a weak partner in the dance of life, God is dying for you to let him lead you and be your ultimate strength. In fact, God *already* died for you, in the weakness of Jesus, to dance *with* you. When you admit your weakness and respect his strength—when you can see how you're Melinda to his Mark—that's when you can gain the strength to let him carry you through life. Like Mark, God is more than strong enough to pick you up regardless of your supposed deficiencies. God is the only *mark* of strength you need.

Keep the image of Mark dancing with Melinda in the back of your mind as we journey together in this chapter. Weakness in community, in essence, is being vulnerable in our weaknesses with others while living out of the amazing truth that God is our strength. When our strength ends, God's begins.

We dance through our weaknesses in three types of relationships: with strangers, with friends, and with our spouse. As the level of intimacy increases from one type of relationship to the next, so too does the opportunity for God to show you your weaknesses.

> Weakness in community, in essence, is being vulnerable in our weaknesses with others while living out of the amazing truth that God is our strength.

Weakness in Community with Strangers

"May I help you with that?"

I've lost count of how many times I've heard that question when I've ambled out of my Jeep to fetch my wheelchair in the back of my Jeep Grand Cherokee. I'm usually at a coffee shop when this happens.

Everyone who knows me knows I love meeting people over coffee. I discovered I had a preference—maybe it was a prejudice—of how I liked to meet people. But I have really always hated the thought of meeting people when I'm getting out of my Jeep and they ask me, "May I help you?"

I get why they're asking me that. If they don't know me, they see a man who's walking like he may have had too many drinks—and I'm not talking about too many mochas. Because of my CP, my walk looks strange to most. It must look like I'm struggling just to get the few feet from my driver's side to the back of the truck. So, very nicely, they ask, "Do you need some help?"

If you've read this far, you know that I seldom want to ask for help. In fact, my first thought after being asked this question was often, *Wow! Do I need help? How do you think I'm planning on getting to the back of my Jeep? I'm sure glad you were waiting for me at the coffee shop and you're willing to help me get my wheelchair out. What else would I have done? Just sat in my car until a Good Samaritan finally asked to help me?*

If that sounds sarcastic and rude, that's because it is. Thankfully, I've never said those things aloud. Well, maybe once or twice a few words slipped out, but the hearer probably couldn't tell what I was saying (a speech impediment has its perks). As nicely as I could, I would decline their offer and (pridefully) show them exactly how this guy with CP could get his own chair out of his own Jeep using his own hands and feet—thank you very much. I was full of pride and ignorant of the blessings that could be experienced by both these strangers I'd rejected and myself, all because I hadn't let them into my weakness.

Eventually, my senior citizen friend Alex reoriented my attitude about accepting help. We'd often meet at a coffee house to play chess and talk about life. Alex would always ask to help me with the door or to get in and out of my car, and I would always decline. After we'd gotten to know each other better, he told me that *everyone* at the shop now knew *not* to ask to help me because I'd been so vocal about not wanting help. Maybe I did have a problem!

But then he spoke the truth in love to me: "Todd, it makes people feel good to help others. The way that I'm made, I'm a helper. It gives me blessings and happiness when I help people. When you say no and are very adamant about not wanting help, you steal the moment of blessing that would come from me being able to help you."

He'd seen right through my strong charade. I didn't want to admit it to myself right then, but I realized he was right. I didn't just shun help from people at coffee shops; I shunned help from *everyone*. I needed to change, both to be blessed and to allow others to be a blessing.

As we kept talking, Alex then said something prophetic: "Todd, when you meet your wife and you start dating, I want you to be open to letting her help you."

I just nodded my head at the time, not knowing how prescient his words would be.

While I didn't automatically start accepting help at the coffee shop, I was impressed by the Spirit to alter my attitude and perspective whenever I heard that inevitable question upon exiting my truck: "May I help you?" Instead of turning the person away and insisting I could do it on my own, I seized the opportunity as a starting point for a relationship. I'd reply, "No thank you, but hey, what's your name? How are you?" Sometimes I'd say, "No, but what can I pray for you about today?" If the Holy Spirit pricked my heart, I'd even say, "Sure! Thank you so much for your help. You can walk with me to the back of my car."

More lasting conversations than I can count have occurred as a result of that simple mindset shift. In fact, I have a friend to this day whom I invested in because we first met when he asked me, "Would you like some help?" Had I never said yes, I would have never been able to experience the blessing of meeting Brandon and building a friendship with him.

We must let ourselves be weak to connect with people. Weakness is the commonality of every human being, an immediate connection that, through transparency and humbleness, the best friendships can be formed and the greatest accomplishments can be experienced. It's only when we publicly admit our need for help and actually allow others to help us in our weakness that true, deep, lasting relationships can begin to grow.

While community can be found with strangers, better bonds grow through the more demanding yet enriching relationships we create with friends. To see friendships thrive, we must learn to likewise reveal our weaknesses to them too.

> Weakness is the commonality of every human being, an immediate connection that, through transparency and humbleness, the best friendships can be formed and the greatest accomplishments can be experienced.

Weakness in Community with Friends

Years ago, seven college friends and I traveled to New York City to explore the city and check off a bucket-list item: celebrate New Year's Eve in Times Square. We spent a week there, but all of us were looking forward to the big party. The night was so cold that my friends tried to sit on me and huddle around me to keep warm. Ten minutes before the ball drop, I had the wild idea that it'd be fun to sing "You've Lost That Lovin' Feelin.'" (I'd just recently watched *Top Gun.*)

If you think I can't talk like others, you should hear me sing! When I sing in the shower, I've often had family members ask me, "Is something wrong? Todd, are you hurt? Are you okay?" Then, rather unnecessarily, they elaborate, "You sound like you're dying in there."

On that New Year's Eve night, I feared no such critics. I belted out the opening lines. By the second line, one of my friends had joined in. By the time we hit the first chorus, it seemed that most of our group was singing along. In a small way, I experienced how friends turn your weakness into strength. Suddenly, people outside of our group started singing. Then, by the time we reached the bridge of the song, it seemed as if a thousand people in our vicinity were all singing with wild abandon. It was incredible and surreal on this famous square in New York City.

But then something even more unbelievable occurred. When the song ended, a woman who seemed to be in her thirties, and at least more than a little inebriated, stumbled toward our group. In her brokenness, emptiness, and weakness that would never be satiated by anything in this world, she asked us to sing "Amazing Grace." We gladly obliged as the new Times Square choir I'd established moments earlier sang out and rang in the new year by celebrating grace—the unmerited favor this lady was longing for and the unmerited favors of experiencing the power of God with friends while bringing in the new year, even through my weak, disfluent singing voice!

> Community transforms weakness into ripples of power. Weakness plus synergy equals impacting lives!

All types of weaknesses exist in a community of friends, but they also provide a host of strengths you'd never have access to alone. Community transforms weakness into ripples of power. Weakness plus synergy equals impacting lives!

I'm reminded of the historical moment when Moses's friends, Aaron and Hur, literally held him up. During a battle between the Israelites and the Amalekites, Moses stood on a hill and held aloft the staff of God.

When Moses held his hand up, that Israel prevailed,
and when he let his hand down, Amalek prevailed. But
Moses' hands were heavy. Then they took a stone and
put it under him, and he sat on it; and Aaron and Hur
supported his hands, one on one side and one on the
other. Thus his hands were steady until the sun set. So
Joshua overwhelmed Amalek and his people with the
edge of the sword. (Exod. 17:11–13)

What an incredible illustration of being weak in community. With God himself and the friends and family he's placed in our lives, he's given us all we need to win the battles of our days. But we have to be willing to show our weakness *and* allow our friends to help us along the way. We weren't made to be lone rangers; we were made to exist together. God's power in weakness is expressed fully in community.

If I hadn't let myself be weak and vulnerable among my friends, our New Year's Eve song would not have begun rippling out into the voices of those around me, and that woman would have never sought us out to ask for a spiritual song in a mostly unspiritual place. That moment is a small-scale depiction of how God uses his community on earth to transform the world through their weaknesses. What begins with the faith of just one person ripples out further than anyone in the group can imagine. In a community of friends, your weakness gets people involved to live lives beyond themselves.

Jesus told the weak disciples that they'd do even greater things than he, because his Spirit would be in many weak vessels and not just one strong and perfect vessel: himself (John 14:12). If Jesus can trust his total work over decades and centuries to a community of weak vessels, who are still accomplishing the task of spreading the good news of Jesus, can't we relinquish and trust community to help us as well? God did so and he's all-powerful! Can't we welcome others into our weakness so they can be our strength? Not only does God trust weak vessels with his tasks, but he also trusts weak vessels with his power to accomplish his tasks.

If all-powerful God can entrust weak people, can you and I, who are also weak people, do the same and trust other weak people?

Weakness among Friends Leads to Power

In the story of the paralytic man being lowered through the roof of a crowded building so that Jesus might heal him, most people focus on the faith of the paralytic man's friends. But have you ever considered the story from the paralytic man's point of view? Did he need faith too?

When they arrived at the crowded house, "they went up on the roof and let him down through the tiles with his stretcher, into the middle of the crowd, in front of Jesus" (Luke 5:19). They could ascend to the roof because ladders or stairs often led to roofs in these Jewish homes. Additionally, removing parts of the roof, likely made of clay or mud, wasn't as difficult as it would be with modern homes. This man's friends were on a mission, and nothing was going to deter them from helping their friend.

But what was the man in the stretcher thinking?

I can place myself in the paralyzed man's sandals, if he even wore any. If I had been him, I wouldn't have wanted my friends to make such a spectacle in order to help me. This is why I often wouldn't let someone just help me get my wheelchair out of my car or open a door for me. I certainly wouldn't want them to physically cart me on a stretcher onto someone's house! I would not have wanted them to do something like that in front of a crowd either.

All eyes on weak me? No thank you!

And I absolutely would not have wanted Jesus, the most famous man of his time and region, to see me in such a pitiful state. I would have wanted to impress him, maybe even to show him how I could take a few steps on my own, or wedge my way toward him all by myself, even in the midst of the crowd. Wouldn't he see more faith that way?

Sadly, if I had been that man, my pride would have taken over. I would not have given those guys the blessing of helping me and witnessing God's power. And I likely wouldn't have experienced the healing that the paralyzed man ultimately did.

But the paralyzed man exercised a different kind of faith than his friends. His faith wasn't as evident as his friends', but it was no less real and essential. To outsiders (and even today's Bible readers), his faith may have appeared weak compared to his friends' "strong" faith. But I would argue that the paralyzed man's faith was much stronger and much more in line with Jesus's upside-down definition of weakness.

The paralyzed man had to be vulnerable and weak to *relinquish* control and *let* his friends lower him through the roof to access Jesus and his amazing power. The man *allowed* his friends to make that spectacle of lowering him into Jesus's room. What did that man physically do that entire time? *Nothing. Absolutely* nothing! Talk about *unmerited favor.* He rested in the confidence of his friends' strength and that Jesus would heal him. He allowed himself to be weak so that he might be made strong.

A paralytic is weak whether they want to be or not; but this paralytic man had to learn to accept his vulnerability. When he did—and maybe he'd done that long before this momentous event—he experienced intimacy with his friends, *and* his friends experienced *purpose* in helping their friend get closer to God. By allowing himself to be lowered, the man experienced Jesus's power. He was forgiven his sins, then he was physically healed—all because, in humility, he trusted his friends and his God with his weakened state.

His weak became his new strong.

The man who was once only known as "that paralyzed guy" is now forever immortalized as "that guy Jesus healed." Even better for him, he *met* Jesus as a result of accepting his frailty among his friends and letting them help him access Jesus and Jesus's power in his weakness.

The only relationship that reveals more weaknesses than close friendships is the one you have (or will have) with your spouse. With no room to hide, your weaknesses will find you out. Instead of fearing being found out, choose to be weak *first*.

Weakness in Community with Your Spouse

In March of 2012, I kept bumping into the same beautiful woman at a few local coffee shops. (No, I wasn't literally bumping into her. I can control my wheelchair! Well, most of the time.) It didn't take long for me to start hoping that I'd bump into her every time I went into a coffee shop. I had been praying for a wife, helpmate, and partner in the gospel for so long that I had to temper my expectations for how this coffee-shop relationship might percolate into something more than just short conversations.

But God knew what he was doing.

The more that Marissa and I talked, the more we learned how much we had in common. In fact, it seems like it only required our shared loves of Jesus, coffee, and missions to quickly escalate our relationship from acquaintances to friends to boyfriend and girlfriend.

I think most guys are floored when the girl of their dreams shows any indication of wanting to date them, let alone *marry* them. I'd always been confident on the surface with females, but when the relationship got closer, insecurity stepped in. I never knew why. If I felt like a woman was becoming romantically interested in me—like Marissa was—I wanted to roll the other way. A friend eventually pointed out to me why I felt that way: subconsciously, I didn't want her to settle for *my* weakness.

The fact that Marissa chose weak, wheelchair-riding, and stuttering me is an earthly depiction of God's great love for me. For someone like me, who'd always had trouble dating because I felt like my CP and my speech disfluency would always prevent me from having a lifelong relationship with a woman, I was overwhelmed by God's grace being revealed to me through Marissa's love for me.

I thought, as the man, I was supposed to be "the strong one," and she was supposed to be "the weak one." In fact, my insecurities about that became so great that I postponed our wedding a few weeks prior to the wedding itself. Again, I found myself wrestling with my weaknesses (and losing the fight).

When I bared my burden to a friend, his short reply immediately changed my outlook: "Todd, she didn't have to say yes." I had never considered that simple fact! She wanted to be with me, not because she thought I needed help, but because *she wanted to be with me.* In wanting to be married to one whom the world sees as weak, Marissa showed me the grace and unmerited favor of God. Marissa said yes to me and to my weaknesses, both visible and invisible. But, really, Marissa knew she was also saying yes to God's power that she witnessed through my weaknesses.

Once, when I introduced Marissa by name to a friend, he responded to her with, "Glad to meet you, Charis."

I thought, *I know I have a speech impediment, but I'm not that disfluent. How did he get Charis from Marissa?*

Turns out, he was speaking a truth about Marissa. *Charis* is the Greek word for *grace*, which means "unmerited favor." It's the same Greek word that fuels the theme of this book: "My grace is all you need. My power works best in weakness" (2 Cor. 12:9 NLT). As I like to say, God fuels his power in us with his *charis*, which is all we need. In community, unmerited favor through relationships precedes the flow of the power of God and his strength in our weaknesses.

It didn't take me long to see and experience that Marissa's gift was helping. But it did take me a while to get used to it. Before meeting her, I was extremely conditioned to do everything on my own. Maybe I wanted to prove to the world that I could do whatever I wanted and that I wasn't as limited as people may think. Maybe I wanted to prove the same thing to myself. But when Marissa entered my life and willfully, joyfully wanted to help me in so many different areas of my life and ministry, I didn't know what to do!

In choosing to believe that Marissa didn't want to be with me, let alone marry me, I had a startling revelation: I was robbing Marissa of the blessings that Moses's friends had experienced, that the paralytic's friends had experienced, and that my friends at Time Square had experienced of God's power in my weaknesses *among community*. It took time for me to realize that I was not going to be the *only* weak one in the marriage.

This biblical truth helped me see the vision of Marissa marrying me in a fresh perspective: "Two are better than one because they have a good return for their labor. For if either of them falls, the one will lift up his companion. But woe to the one who falls when there is not another to lift him up" (Eccles. 4:9–10). To say that I have fallen a lot in my life while trying to walk is an understatement. You could even say that I'm a professional faller!

But, in our marriage, could it be possible that I wouldn't be the only weak one who falls? Could it be possible that Marissa will be weak at times too, and *I'll* get the blessing of being her strength?

That's when the light bulb went off: It will be a joy for me to bear her weaknesses—why would I want to rob her of that joy?

Would I let my insecurities rob Marissa of the joy of bearing my weaknesses?

Not at all! I would never want to be robbed of getting to carry her in her weaknesses.

Together, as two weaklings in need of Christ and ready to bear each other's burdens, we got married!

Circles of Community

Prior to meeting me, Marissa admitted to being much more introverted than I am. (I am definitely *not* an introvert.) She only went deep with a few friends and seldom got out of her comfort zone to meet others.

But that changed after the birth of our son.

Oliver, our pride and joy, was a high-needs baby. He always, always, *always* needed attention. (Maybe he got that from his dad.) High-needs kids are characterized by perceived weaknesses such as intensity and hyperactivity, and they can be draining, demanding, easily unsatisfied, unpredictable, and highly sensitive.[1] Every child requires attention; Ollie just needed more than most.

As he was first child, we had to learn to be parents as well as caretakers of a high-needs boy. I was and still am constantly amazed at Marissa's love, kindness, and patience when Oliver can be demanding. I wasn't surprised by how she loved him, but I was almost shocked when she told me what she wanted to do shortly after we realized Oliver's weakness of being high-needs.

"I'd like to start a community group for moms with high-needs kids."

Soon after that, she began that community group, which reaches moms with high-needs kids around the Metroplex. Through Marissa choosing to get outside of her comfort zone and to live by God's power beyond her weaknesses, these women are receiving glimpses of Jesus's strength in the weakness of raising their high-needs children.

She wasn't only suggesting helping moms in their weaknesses, but she started a community for moms to help each other in bearing the weaknesses and burdens of raising high-needs children. Basically, she created a weakness-bearing community! In a way, her desire to lead this group of strangers, who then became friends, and was partially birthed from witnessing the power of weakness in her spouse, brought the community of weakness full circle. She was living out this truth: "Now we who are strong ought to bear the weaknesses of those without strength and not just please ourselves" (Rom. 15:1).

One reason she chose to start the community was due to my strengths encouraging her weaknesses. She told me, "Todd, I wouldn't be doing any of this if I didn't see you doing this over time." I was floored. She had allowed my strength to buoy her weakness. In the dance of our ministry, she'd seen me lead through my weakness in intentionality, so she knew what steps to take to lead others in her weakness. Through this experience, I learned that we help each other. Where I am weak, she's strong. Where she's weak, I'm strong. Where we're both weak, God is strong.

The human heart often longs to say yes to bear a loved one's weakness, but that same human heart is often just as reluctant to allow their weaknesses to be borne by another. In other words, I wanted to carry her, to lead our dance, but I first had to learn how to be carried in my weaknesses. I had to allow myself to be helped by someone who wanted to be blessed by bearing my weaknesses. Marriage is a constant yes to bearing each other's weaknesses and encouraging each other to let God be the source of strength.

In Jesus, God willingly became weak to say yes to our weaknesses. Marissa's "yes" to my weaknesses daily reminds me of that truth. I also see how she is blessed by her yes. Likewise, I believe God is blessed by *his* yes to bearing our weaknesses. In a similar way to how Marissa's unconditional love for me drives her to want to shoulder my burdens of weakness with me, so too does God's love long to bear your weaknesses. When you allow yourself to become vulnerable in the intimate community of your marriage, you and your spouse will thrive. When both people in the marriage can allow their weaknesses to be seen, shared, and shouldered, God reveals his power. God delights in revealing his strength within the shared weaknesses of your marriage.

You may already be allowing Jesus to carry you in your weakness, but will you let yourself be carried by the most important person in your life?

How's Your Dancing?

Remember Melinda and Mark's dance? For God to carry you, you must be vulnerable and let yourself be weak. To access strength, you must acknowledge your weakness and be vulnerable among community. In your community among strangers, with your friends, and especially in your marriage, you will find ample opportunities to realize and admit your weaknesses.

Share your weaknesses with people in your life. You'll experience God's strength in community and deep relationships.

Note

[1] Bill Sears, "12 Signs Your Baby Is High Need," Ask Dr Sears, accessed September 5, 2019, https://www.askdrsears.com/topics/health-concerns/fussy-baby/high-need-baby/12-features-high-need-baby/.

CHAPTER 10

PASS ON THE POWER

"For indeed He was crucified because of weakness,
yet He lives because of the power of God.
For we also are weak in Him, yet we will live with Him
because of the power of God directed toward you."
—2 Corinthians 13:4

I'll never forget where I was at 9:03 a.m. on April 19, 1995: rolling out of the Price School of Business on the University of Oklahoma campus in Norman, twenty-four miles away from one of our most tragic instances of domestic terrorism. I felt the ground shake from the reverberations of one man's decision to explode a federal building in downtown Oklahoma City. I couldn't believe the fallout of that one event, both in how I felt its aftershock and how the world experienced its aftermath for decades.

My mom spent nearly twenty years—most of her career—serving the families of the victims of the Oklahoma City bombing. During her career, she journeyed with victims and survivors and listened to hundreds of stories about "that day." Then she worked with these men and women to help them tell their stories and amass artifacts. Eventually, she became the staff liaison for the

Conscience Committee—a group that was formed to ensure that the voices of those lost in the bombing wouldn't be lost forever.

My mother embodies 2 Corinthians 13:4. She understood that "we also are weak with him, yet will we live with him." She is a prime example of how one person can pass on God's power through weaknesses. The strength she received in her life with Christ, she gladly passed on to others in their times of deep grief and greatest need. Christ-followers are all to likewise pass this power on through investing in others and sharing about God's power through their weaknesses so they can then pass it on to people they know. It's a mission that began with our God choosing to weaken himself in order to strengthen us, and it's a mission that will continue through us until Jesus returns.

The impoverished, mourning spirits affected by the Oklahoma City bombing received hope as the nation came together during that tragedy. The bombing not only weakened victims' families, the state and nation also felt weak and vulnerable. But the strength of the city pulling together to help victims' families rippled throughout Oklahoma as the state united around helping the weakened. Those ripples of strength in shared weakness did not stop with Oklahomans. The strength passed on and rippled throughout the nation.

The power of explosive devices to radically alter reality cannot be denied. In the same way, power has been perverted by the world and used for selfish gain, but God's power is pure. The same power that created heaven and earth, the same power that heals the sick through Jesus, the same power that raised Jesus from the dead now resides in you (Eph. 1:19). You see, the gospel is the power of God (Rom. 1:16), and the Greek term that is translated "power" in English is the word *dunamis*. But the *dunamis* of God is not like the dynamite of our world. Instead, God's power in the Bible pulls together, unites, and makes whole. All too often, power has been used like dynamite—as a weapon to destroy, disunite, and pull apart. But God has a different plan. He chooses your weaknesses as his vehicle, a shipping truck, to carry his uniting, holistic power through to impact the world with the good news of Jesus!

God chooses to place his power in jars of clay (2 Cor. 4:7); his surpassing, dynamic power travels through us and lives within our weakness. I write *travels* because this power *exerts* itself, and this is where we get our word *exercise.* God's power *exercises* through us to other people!

To experience this power, we must keep exercising it! If I did not stay mobile, my disability would digress. But I stay mobile, so I'm *always* progressing. God's power becomes explosive through passing it on. It ripples from one person to the next, then from one community to the next. The more I speak into someone's life that their weakness is a vehicle of God's power, the more I'm passionate, convicted, and empowered to live by God's power through my own weaknesses.

> The more I speak into someone's life that their weakness is a vehicle of God's power, the more I'm passionate, convicted, and empowered to live by God's power through my own weaknesses.

This "passing it on" prayer explains it well: "I pray that you may be active in sharing your faith, so that you will have a full understanding of every good thing we have in Christ" (Philem. 1:6 NIV 84). In the same way, I have experienced firsthand that the more I pass on the good news that weakness is a vehicle for God's power through which to travel, the more I let my weaknesses be used as a conduit of God's power.

The Greek word *dunamis* is twice used in 2 Corinthians 12:9, and note its existence *within* weakness: "And He has said to me,

'My grace is sufficient for you, for *power* is perfected in weakness.' Most gladly, therefore, I will rather boast about my weaknesses, so that the *power* of Christ may dwell in me" (emphasis mine).

In contrast, Paul uses the Greek word *krataioō* in Ephesians 3:16 when he prays "that [God] would grant you, according to the riches of His glory, to be *strengthened* with power through His Spirit in the inner man" (emphasis mine).[1] Why do I make this distinction?

Dunamis is the deep, inner power we *already* possess from the Holy Spirit because he lives within us: weak vessels. *Krataioō* refers to the strength we're given as a result of the Holy Spirit and his power. In other words, we are strengthened with the power we already possess through Jesus Christ. How amazing is that? We have inherent, permanent power residing within us! If God has decided to move his power to live within our weak vessels, we are called to exercise it. He has fully entrusted you with his power in your weaknesses to be his representative on earth.

So what are you going to do with your *dunamis*?

- Bury it
- Exercise it and pass it on

I propose that you are made to exercise it and pass it on. But, if you've already buried it, remember:

> You are the light of the world. A city set on a hill cannot be hidden; nor does anyone light a lamp and put it under a basket, but on the lampstand, and it gives light to all who are in the house. Let your light shine before men in such a way that they may see your good works, and glorify your Father who is in heaven. (Matt. 5:14–16)

Unlike the disastrous ways that dynamite can be used, we've been given pure power, a much more positive manner of dynamiting our world. But the way of God's Spirit is not a short-fused explosive that burns hot and leaves a crater. Instead, the power of God is a dynamic energy that creates community through our yielded and frail bodies.

Recently, I moved to Hollywood, California; but for forty-five years, I lived in Texas and Oklahoma. One thing Californians immediately notice is that I use the word "y'all." No matter how hard I try to not say "y'all," I can't help it. Talking Texan, oh so inelo-quently with my speech impediment, is my natural way to mention "you" when it's a plural. In all the passages that I've mentioned so far, we find the word "y'all." Paul's prayer is that y'all would be strength-ened in y'all's inner being; and Jesus is saying, "y'all are the light of the world." God is hoping that his treasure in a jar of clay will find synergy as we shine out together. Jesus's goal is not for us to be single lights that shine alone. We, together, are the light of the world.

Our job on earth is to pass on his power to other weak vessels. Passing this power is in God's DNA! He longs to turn your weaknesses into *dunamis*. Your weakness is your major, invaluable resource in accessing God's power. When you can admit where you're weak, God can then reveal your true strength. In fact, God wants his power to flow through your weakness until he uses his power to *heal* your weakness—whether God's healing takes place during this life or when you're with him after you pass away from this earth. But your job remains the same: pass on God's power to others!

God may heal me by the time you read this book. While you're reading this, I might be playing football with my son or be a voice-over artist with no slurring. But I will *still* have other weaknesses. I'm going to decide now to give those to God to be a conduit of his power. I'm deciding now to invest in the lives of others by passing on the power to those in my life so they can live in victory with their weaknesses!

As the Spider-Man movies have famously said, "With great power comes great responsibility." In knowing that God's power in your life is found within living out of your weaknesses, you now have great responsibility! When your weakness is your strength, you are commissioned to mentor others to experience God's power through their weaknesses. Not only is your weakness a conduit of God's power, now you can reproduce that power by mobilizing others so they can also reveal God's power through their weaknesses to others. Pass on the power!

From Weakness to Weakness to . . . Strength

Have you ever noticed how God passes his power on through weaker and weaker states?

First, God has always existed as an all-powerful ruler on his throne. Then, just as we started this journey together in Chapter One, he stepped off his throne and became a little weaker as human in the flesh. In Jesus, all that power was somehow temporarily contained in the weakest vessel known to man: a baby! Then Jesus subjected himself to the severe limitations of living in the flesh, like forgoing the ability to be omnipresent.

Then Christ allowed himself to become even weaker on the cross. Betrayed, whipped, crowned with thorns, burdened by a cross, and thrust through with a spear, Jesus bled blood and water, which caused his body to become even weaker than a child's. If weakness is really strength, this is when the "passing on" is really on. Yet Christ still had one more weak state to endure: death. And, incredibly, he willingly allowed himself to die, though he could have called ten thousand angels to his rescue. Is there anything weaker than a dead man?

But three days later, he was resurrected in *power*, becoming human flesh again—yet this time, he was victorious over death. Then he passed on that same power and victory to us: "'O DEATH,

WHERE IS YOUR VICTORY? O DEATH, WHERE IS YOUR STING?' The sting of death is sin, and the power of sin is the law; but thanks be to God, who gives us the victory through our Lord Jesus Christ" (1 Cor. 15:55–57). God began with power then died in weakness, only to be raised in power. Now, the power is passed, and God's power resides in all his vessels!

> God began with power then died in weakness, only to be raised in power. Now, the power is passed, and God's power resides in all his vessels!

We desperately need this power because even "the weakness of God is stronger than men" (1 Cor. 1:25). If our strongest efforts are *nothing* compared to God's weaknesses, imagine how our weaknesses compare to God's strengths. Even having God's "least" is more than enough for us!

This power lives out its vocational work within us: "Now to Him who is able to do far more abundantly beyond all that we ask or think, according to the power that works within us" (Eph. 3:20). This is my new life verse, both for its promise and its premise. I believe God *will* do "more abundantly" because I've experienced his abundance in my life. But I've also experienced "the power that works within us" so deeply that when I say I'm thankful for my weakness, I mean it! I realize the truth of 2 Corinthians 12:9, that his power *is* perfected in *my* weakness! My cerebral palsy doesn't hold me back; it's my strength for living a life worthy of the calling God has placed on me.

Now I live not according to my weakness, but according to God's dynamic, *dunamis* power. The power of the God, who created the universe, lives within you and me; therefore, in Christ, life is without limits. And it's not like it's a dormant inhabitant of my heart; rather, his power daily works to shape my life and identity. Now I live a life beyond myself. I don't live according to my weaknesses *or* my strengths. I live according to the power of God. And I live knowing that God has given me—given us—this power so that we might pass it on.

Passing the Power One-to-One

It blows my mind that the Holy Spirit placed some books within the Bible that began simply as letters from one person to another— all literal representations of passing on the power! These letters show how God grows something enormous from something small: one-to-one relationships. From the time the letter was written until today, one-on-one discipleship has led the way.

Paul's letters to his young disciple Timothy are like an impacting discipleship meeting put on paper. I feel an empathy with Paul, because my career has mostly been about mentoring and making disciples one-on-one just like that (but in coffee shops), with the vision of seeing *them* likewise disciple people they know—to pass it on. And just like I speak identity into those I meet with, Paul reminds Timothy of the power of God that resided within him: "For God has not given us a spirit of fear and timidity, but of power, love, and self-discipline" (2 Tim. 1:7 NLT).

How fascinating that *power* is one of the three agents Paul wanted Timothy to know God had given him. This is overlooked today because power has been so abused and misused. It's time for God's people to redeem power! It's time for us to live in confidence that we are powerful people because God chose weakness to be a conduit of that power. And now, it's time to pass on the power.

Paul then encourages Timothy: "The things which you have heard from me in the presence of many witnesses, entrust these to faithful men who will be able to teach others also" (2 Tim. 2:2). I pray that you'll catch this grand vision of passing on the good news of God's power flowing through your weaknesses to the people in your life.

But the vision is even grander: these people will pass on the power as well! In this one verse, passing the power occurs in five spiritual generations:

1. Paul passes on the power to Timothy.
2. Paul passes on the power to many witnesses.
3. Many witnesses pass on the power.
4. "Other trustworthy people" pass on the power.
5. "Others" will pass on the power.

This verse also shows how multifaceted the passing on of God's power is: God's power in weakness ripples through a larger community as well as through intimate, one-on-one relationships like the one Paul and Timothy had.

A Weak Man Discipling a Strong Man

When it comes to memorable one-on-one relationships, and especially when the word "power" is used, I think of Logan. I still remember the first time I met him. Anyone would have. He's huge. I'm pretty sure his muscles have muscles. When he first started attending a Bible study I led at the University of North Texas, I made a mental note not to anger him (even though I later found out I *couldn't* anger this Christ-infused teddy bear). He looked like he could pick me and my wheelchair up with one finger. (That may be an exaggeration. Then again, I never asked him to try.)

He was a weightlifter—and not just for a hobby. After we met, he became the Collegiate National Powerlifting Champion, which had qualified him for a World Powerlifting competition. I journeyed with him while he was working his way toward competing on the world stage. He was determined to be the best weightlifter in the world. He was also determined to learn more about Jesus, and I was glad to be his coach in that respect.

A few months into our Bible study, Logan suffered such an intense hernia while lifting that he could hardly walk because of the pain. It was devastating for his advancement toward the world weightlifting competition. When he shared his setback with our Bible study, I asked our group to pray for Logan's healing, believing that when Jesus said the faith of a mustard seed could result in an incomparably large return, he meant it.

The following week, despite his doctors saying that he'd need serious surgery before resuming his passion, Logan told our group that he'd been able to resume lifting the same amount of weight as he had just prior to his injury. Our group realized that you didn't have to have faith as large as Logan's muscles to experience answered prayers. You just needed mustard-seed faith.

Remember how *dunamis* is the power of God "exercising" through our weaknesses? I witnessed a physical illustration of that exerted, exercising power when, after God healed Logan, Logan launched the first kettlebell training on campus at UNT. He seemed to have come back stronger and more determined following his injury.

But that's not the end of the story; and if you're living to pass on the power of God's strength in your weakness, it seldom ever is.

As Logan wrote on our Mobilize Ministries™ website:

> For two years Todd ministered to me one-on-one and to this day, when I share my continually lengthening God story, he is always included as one of the pivotal figures God had cast in this epic drama of the ages. I don't take lightly the spiritual encouragement God brought me through Todd, especially during those darker days of my journey through the wilderness. Todd built my faith every time we met. He continually reminded me of the abundance of God's grace. How I have been made clean

in His sight. Who we are positionally in Christ. That
we have been made complete in Him. That I have been
transferred from the kingdom of darkness into the kingdom of Light and now an official ambassador for Christ
and His Kingdom. This was the best news I had ever
heard and has affected my ministry greatly, in that it's all
reproducible—disciples who make disciples.[2]

As much as it thrills me to read about Logan's spiritual growth
during our time together, it's that last line that makes me know he
gets it. As Christ-followers, we not only live to help others know
and love God, but we cast the vision for them to do the same with
the individuals in their lives—to pass on the power. I would later
discover that Logan wasn't just talking the Christian talk; he was
walking the Christian walk too.

A year later, Marissa and I began our ministry among young
professionals in a different city: the Dallas-Fort Worth Metroplex.
During one of my routine coffee shop mornings, a young man
walked in, saw me, walked directly toward me, and asked, "Are
you Todd Lollar?"

I didn't know the guy or how he could have known me. Before
I could get a word out, he continued speaking. "There's a guy
named Logan that discipled me, and I'm pretty sure you're my
spiritual granddad."

I smiled as widely as I could and embraced him as my spiritual grandson.

This is the power of weakness multiplying itself through
others likewise choosing to make themselves weak. This is how
the one-on-one investment of your life into another soul results
in multiple spiritual generations. This is how God's community
was sparked, continues to flame, and will continue to explode
through weak vessels.

This is how the kingdom grows: not through muscles and might, but through faith and obedience—through passing on the power from one weak person to the next.

Are You Passing On the Power?

Some of you may be thinking, *I'd love to disciple others, but I don't have* _____. That blank could be filled by any number of apparent weaknesses:

- "I don't have time."
- "I don't have people skills."
- "I don't have deep biblical knowledge."

Those may all be true for you, but they shouldn't prevent you from discipling others. God wants to flow his power through these vehicles of weaknesses too!

For example, my son Oliver was born with the inability to have children. He's too young to understand the ramifications of his body not being able to produce testosterone, but I'm not. His physical "weakness" could mean that Marissa and I never receive the joy of being grandparents through him. But if we take such a limited view of his limitations, we're missing the bigger picture. In fact, if we allowed ourselves to believe that his "weakness" would prevent him from ever enjoying being a father, we may even be limiting God's plans for his life.

I have hope for being a grandfather through Oliver (many years from now!) for two reasons. First, I can't help but envision the children that our Oliver will save through fostering and adopting. If he's forever saddled with the physical inability to produce children of his own, he can still have children in whom he invests his life, and they will be his children as much as Oliver is our child.

Second, just as I know that God can 100 percent heal me, I know he can 100 percent heal Oliver too. But believing and asking and praying for Oliver's healing doesn't change what God can do for him and through him in the meantime. His weaknesses are not useless to God! (Neither are yours!) We are never "in waiting." My son will still be used by God. As I will encourage him, so too do I encourage you: "You are from God, little children, and have overcome them; because greater is He who is in you than he who is in the world" (1 John 4:4). Oliver needs someone (like his father) to pass on the power to him. He needs me to tell him and show him that God will use his weaknesses as a conduit of God's power. He'll get to experience the blessing of passing this message on to his younger siblings, his friends, his future spouse, and children.

That's what I'm challenging you to do too.

Maybe you *don't* have enough time to invest in others. If that's true, what can you sacrifice (TV, games, social media, sports, etc.) to make room for one-on-one mentoring?

If you don't have people skills, how can you learn them? Maybe this is an opportunity for God's power to pass through your weakness.

And if you feel that you lack biblical knowledge, realize God will use your daily walk with him, your daily quiet time in his word, and the daily experience his Spirit gives to you to pass on to someone you know. Do you know that weakness you have that God uses to flow his power through? I know you do. Pass on the hope you have that your weaknesses are not useless—they are a conduit for God's power!

Ultimately, the question you should ask yourself is: To whom am I passing the power today?

This is our calling. God has empowered us in our weaknesses to be his heart, hands, and feet made real to the people around us.

The Model of Passing On the Power

Do you now believe that weak is the new strong?

Will you revel in your weakness and delight in your frailties, and encourage a friend to do the same?

Will you praise God for your shortcomings and thank him for your lack, and invite family to praise and thank God with you in their deficiencies?

Will you turn over what little you have so that he might make much of it, and share this investment strategy with one who needs financial freedom?

Will you empower someone with the ultimate power, teaching him or her that God *loves* to use weak people just like you and me?

> Jesus experienced your weakness on the cross, but then he set you up for hope, for victory, for power!

Jesus experienced your weakness on the cross, but then he set you up for hope, for victory, for power! Through his life, ministry, death, and resurrection, he modeled how we ought to pass on his power to others.

See how God passes his power to us: "For indeed He was crucified because of weakness, yet He lives because of the power of God. *For we also are weak in Him, yet we will live with Him because of the power of God directed toward you*" (2 Cor. 13:4—emphasis mine). Before "the pass," when Jesus passed his power on to us, Jesus was just as weak as we are. He lived within a frail body that could be hurt and killed, and he *was* brutally hurt and famously killed on a cross. But in the most incredible reversal of the accepted truth that strength rules the world, God used Jesus's voluntary weakness to *conquer* our greatest weaknesses: sin and death.

But if Jesus, after his resurrection, resumed his all-powerful state after allowing himself to become so weak, how could we "yet live with Him" (2 Cor. 13:4)? How can weaklings like me, like you, and like everyone else on earth have a relationship with the God of the universe?

"Because of the power of God directed toward *you*" and me! When he defeated death on Friday, our weakest state as humans, he passed that power on to us through his resurrection on Sunday. This Sunday "pass" is better than any throw on a Super Bowl Sunday. Jesus passed his power *to us*!

Once you realize this, your life must then answer a single question: To whom will you pass on the power so he or she will experience the power Jesus passed to us? Live and speak in such a way that you empower your family, friends, coworkers, and even complete strangers to release and pass on his power to someone else's weaknesses!

Stop believing it's Friday! It *was* Friday, but Sunday is *here*! Christ lives! And not only that, Christ lives *in you*, no matter how weak you are. And you have the divine purpose to pass on his power to weak family and friends.

I know this because I'm one of the "weakest" people I know, but I can't deny how God's power has changed my life and how I've seen his power through me change others' lives. Today, I'm the executive director of the nationwide nonprofit I founded: Mobilize Ministries™. Upon writing this book, we've expanded Mobilize Ministries™ from Dallas to Hollywood among the entertainment industry. I love mobilizing people in their callings! It's my hope and prayer that these words will likewise motivate you to mobilize others to live out God's power through their weaknesses!

With due respect to S. M. Lockridge's rousing sermon that's come to be known as "It's Friday," here's my take:

It's Friday. Just born, I'm barely breathing. Mom's a-praying. My heart's hardly beating. But Sunday's comin'.

It's Friday. Can't walk, can't talk. Legs and tongue imprisoned, just like my heart. But Sunday's comin'.

It's Friday. Willie's laughing, Mary's poor. Satan's tormenting me as I roll through the doors. But Sunday's comin'.

It's Friday. I'm dejected after rejection from job after job. I wonder if this is really my calling from God. But Sunday's comin'.

It's Friday. I'm rolling through a crowd to seek the answer to my prayers, but, about this trifling issue, I'm doubting God really cares. But Sunday's comin'.

It's Friday. The frat doesn't realize who they are and Haiti is too poor. A church wants to split as I pray on the floor. But Sunday's comin'.

It's Friday. The prof. says I'll never earn a master's. I'm self-conscious about my speech. I'm doubting God (again) with whether he can use someone like me. But Sunday's comin'.

It's Friday. Everywhere I look, all I see is what I lack. But Sunday's comin'.

It's Friday. "Do you need help with that?" echoes in my ears. "No, I can do it," is all they get to hear. But Sunday's comin'.

It's Friday. I *still* have CP, still can't talk as fast as my mind moves, and still have to use a wheelchair. But Sunday's comin'.

It's Friday, but Sunday . . . already came!

On that Friday two thousand years ago, Jesus died in weakness so he could rise in the power of God and pass it on to you! Now it's your turn. To whom will you pass on the power that God flows through your weaknesses? You know they have weaknesses too.

Give them the opportunity to pass on the power!

Notes

[1] "Lexicon: Strong's G2901–*krataioō*," *Blue Letter Bible*, s.v., "κραταιόω," https://www.blueletterbible.org/lang/lexicon/lexicon.cfm?Strongs=G2901&t =NASB.

[2] Logan Nyquist, "Todd & Logan's Journey: Student, Friend, Supporter," *ToddLollar.com* (blog) October 7, 2018, https://www.toddlollar.com/2018/10 /logans-discipleship-journey-with-todd-now-monthly-supporter/.